*6 ...*

# Living Deeply

*12*

# Living Deeply

## A Psychological and Spiritual Journey

Fraser Watts

The Lutterworth Press

*To John Marks*

**The Lutterworth Press**
P.O. Box 60
Cambridge
CB1 2NT
United Kingdom

www.lutterworth.com
publishing@lutterworth.com

ISBN: 978 0 7188 9512 9

*British Library Cataloguing in Publication Data*
A record is available from the British Library

First published by The Lutterworth Press, 2018

# Contents

## Section Three
*Going Deeper*

# Acknowledgements

I am immensely grateful to John Marks for his support of the Beta Course, on which this book is partly based, and to the Mulberry Trust for their support of the *Living Deeply* project. Also to my colleagues, especially Sara Savage who co-ordinated the Beta Course and who has helped with *Living Deeply*, and also to Roger Bretherton and Nick Devenish. I am also aware of how indebted I am to Stephen Verney who for many years was such a great inspiration and who helped me to understand what Christianity is all about.

# Foreword

Many people these days are interested in following a spiritual path of some kind. This book is for such people.

My own background is in the Christian tradition, and I draw on that here. However, I want this book to be useful both to those who identify themselves as Christians, and to those who are merely interested in the Christian path amongst others. I have tried to write in a way that does not presuppose any religious beliefs or commitments. I hope this book will be read, not only by Christians, but by people who adhere to other faith traditions such as Buddhism, people interested in 'new age', people practising mindfulness, and by many others.

Throughout this book, I have kept psychology in play as a partner in the dialogue. That opens up space and avoids religion taking over, as religion tends to do. I increasingly feel that religion needs to be in dialogue with some other perspective. If religion has the stage to itself, it tends to become over-dogmatic, and then it goes bad.

This is another way of recognising a point that has often been made in more traditional language, that 'spiritual pride' is one of the worst 'sins' and that, when religious people become arrogant and closed-minded, the good in what they are trying to do becomes corrupted. Religion seems to need a larger context, and then it can be marvellously life-giving. I think Jesus was making a similar point when he said that the kingdom of Heaven is like yeast (Matthew 13:33).

There are various possible conversation partners for religion and spirituality (such as science or poetry), but I think there is a special place for psychology. Some years ago I was approached by a retired businessman, John Marks, who wanted to bring Christianity and psychology closer together, and sought my help with that. *Living Deeply* is a long-term offshoot of our collaboration. John's infectious enthusiasm made him very lovable, and I am pleased to dedicate this book to him.

John's reason for wanting to bring Christianity and psychology together was simple and compelling. As he saw it, Christianity is about personal transformation; and psychology is the discipline devoted to understanding how people change. So, if Christianity is to help people to actually change, it needs the perspective of psychology to help it to do that more effectively. I agreed with John about that, and still do.

It is worth noting here that psychology and Christianity are playing different roles. Christianity, like any other spiritual approach, has a distinct point of view. It has a particular framework for understanding things, specific objectives, and a distinct set of practices designed to bring them about. Psychology is more general. It takes an overall view of how people function, why they behave as they do, how they change etc. It is an overall approach that can be applied to anything concerning people, including Christianity and other spiritual paths.

In chapter one I focus on the inner journey, a journey that is partly spiritual and partly psychological. Neither approach captures the journey adequately, but together they reflect its richness and complexity, more than either approach can do alone. Psychology can provide a neutral and more accessible language for talking about what are essentially spiritual matters. I would not want to say that religion can be translated entirely into psychology, but it often helps to put spiritual things in psychological terms, where that is possible. Over the last hundred years there has been an astonishing growth in familiarity with psychology, and a corresponding decline in familiarity with religion, so psychology has now become the more accessible language.

The general direction of travel in this book is from the psychological to the religious. I deliberately start from psychology, because it is the more accessible approach. However, as the book goes on, I make increasing use of religious perspectives and go deeper into spirituality.

Section One starts from psychology and deals with various important personal issues, such as coping with stress. Depression is particularly interesting because all areas of human life are affected. Spiritual aspects are important too, and they have often been neglected. Loss is something that everyone has to cope with at some time or other, and it is an issue that Christianity has a lot to say about. Finally, in this section, I look at the twin themes of suffering and wholeness. Again, I draw on psychology as I explore how people find meaning in suffering, how they can find healing, and what 'wholeness' means in practice.

In each case, spiritual practices can make a useful contribution to coping, and I conclude each chapter with a spiritual perspective after first taking a broader look at coping strategies. My general claim is that spiritual approaches to coping can go beyond other coping approaches. They add something distinctive and are not just more of the same.

Then in Section Two I broaden out to look at the relational and social context. We live in an age in which people tend to exaggerate the extent to which people are 'individuals'. I emphasise here the extent to which relationships are a crucial part of every human life. They are not an 'add-on', but fundamental. And it is not only one-to-one relationships that are important; the sense of being part of a community is important too. Some people think that psychology is purely individualistic, but it includes a social perspective and recognises the importance of relationships and community.

Again there are important religious angles. Forgiveness is probably the most important religious approach to sorting out tangled relationships and can make an important contribution, both to one-to-one relationships and to relationships between groups and nations. Forgiveness occupies an interesting place in the interface between psychology and religion. Its origins are in religion but it has recently migrated across into psychology (rather like mindfulness) and become secularised. There are thus both psychological and religious approaches to forgiveness and they have different emphases, which are interesting to compare.

Section Three draws more fully on religion and spirituality. I start with various reasons, both intuitive and scientific, for thinking that there is something more than the apparently material world that we see around us, and begin to explore what is involved in thinking of that something more as God. I focus then on a particularly important issue in how people understand both themselves and religious traditions such as Christianity, i.e. darkness and light.

Most things in life are both good and bad, and have both light and dark elements that are intertwined. That is sometimes hard for us to cope with; we tend to lapse into 'splitting', seeing some things as entirely good and others as entirely bad. That is often a problem in how we see ourselves and others. It is also an important issue in religious thinking. In fact I increasingly feel that the most important difference between healthy and unhealthy forms of religion is whether they recognise that good and evil are intertwined. Religious thinking is most dangerous when it fails to recognise that.

The next two chapters are the most explicitly Christian, and I turn to focus on Jesus. Despite increasing scepticism about 'God', most people continue to have a very positive view of Jesus, though people's understanding of him is, to my mind, often too much influenced by what church people think, rather than by the historical records in the New Testament and elsewhere. I try to focus down on what Jesus actually said and did. When it comes to making claims about Jesus, I put the emphasis on what he accomplished rather than who and what he was; and I argue that in doing so I am being faithful to the New Testament.

Then I consider traditional ideas about 'sin' and 'salvation', and explore what they mean at a human level, making use of ideas drawn from psychology. Christians have always allowed various different ideas about what Jesus accomplished to run side by side, and I try to introduce some new ideas into the discussion drawing, for example, ideas from photosynthesis and family systems. I take a strong view of the importance of Jesus for the future course of the whole of humanity, not just for 'believers'.

Finally, I talk explicitly about God. I am aware that the idea of 'God' is now often a stumbling block to people following a religious path, though often people struggle over a concept of God that is not necessarily held by religiously committed people. The solution seems to me to focus on the reality of God, as God is actually experienced, and to rise above words and concepts that are necessarily limited, and sometimes misleading. In this section I also try to tackle the complex relationship between God and ourselves. As I see it, there are two opposing pitfalls to be avoided here. One is that God is nothing more than ourselves; the other is that there is necessarily an opposition between God and ourselves. The middle path recognises the close connection between God and what is best in ourselves, but doesn't identify that with God entirely.

The first two sections of the book are closely connected with the first two modules of the film clips of *Living Deeply* that are available for free computer download (from the Cambridge Institute for Applied Psychology and Religion), though they develop the material beyond what is available on those films. The third module in the film clips, which is more spiritual and religious, is scattered around here. One session, 'Suffering and Wholeness', is now to be found at the end of Section One. The other two sessions of module three of the film clips are at the end of Section Three of this book, and follow three entirely new chapters.

Some readers will want to know how the material here relates to the Bible, which is a touchstone of Christian wisdom. The ideas presented in this book have been developed through a dialogue between psychology and religion in which the Bible has played a crucial role. I have indicated some of the key connections in the text, but at the end of every chapter I have included a special section of Bible passages suggested for study.

The Old Testament includes many key stories in which much human life is to be seen in all its richness and complexity. They don't deal explicitly with psychological ideas, but they describe events in human lives that are of much psychological interest. One of the best examples is the story of Joseph. My colleague, Sara Savage, has written a book about the story of Joseph[1] that explicitly connects with many of the topics covered in Sections One and Two of this book, drawing on material in an earlier form of *Living Deeply* known as the 'Beta Course'. I recommend her book very enthusiastically. She covers the topics in a slightly different order from how they appear here, but that is dictated by the series of events in the story of Joseph.

I hope that many readers will want to think over how the material here relates to themselves and the personal issues they face. I have provided a question for discussion at the end of each section to help with that. If you read this book in a group of other people, those questions would provide a basis for group discussion.

1.  Sara Savage (2011) *Joseph: Insights for the Spiritual Journey.* SPCK.

Some readers will want to go more deeply into the material here, and at the end of each chapter I have also provided some guidance where to go for that. It is also an opportunity to give an indication of some of the material on which I have drawn. I have generally tried to avoid the academic habit of constantly referencing my sources. However, there is a strong basis in scholarship for most of the material presented here, even though I have sometimes been path-breaking in the way I have linked up psychology and spirituality. There are two books of my own that connect with this book at many points and may be useful companions. One, written with colleagues, is about the contribution of psychology to Christian ministry.[1] The other, my most recent book, is an overview of what psychology has to say about religion and spirituality.[2]

Naturally, I hope that people will find this book interesting. Words convey ideas, so writing a book necessarily engages at the level of ideas. But there is more to life than words and ideas. Though they are necessarily the vehicle of my engagement with my readers, I hope for a broader engagement. My hope is that this book will affect what people do and what they experience, as well as what they think. Indeed, my immodest ambition is that people will be changed by reading this book.

---

1. Fraser Watts, Rebecca Nye and Sara Savage (2002) *Psychology for Christian Ministry*. Routledge.
2. Fraser Watts (2017) *Psychology, Religion and Spirituality*. Cambridge University Press.

# Chapter One
## *The Inner Journey*

## Perspectives from Psychology and Spirituality

I want to start by speaking about the journey inwards. Throughout this book, I will draw on the perspectives of both psychology and spirituality. I believe it will help us to keep both perspectives in play; it gives us a kind of 'binocular vision' on this journey. Looked at in one way, it is a psychological journey of personal growth. Looked at in another way, it is a journey into greater spiritual depth. Because it is both of these things, we can miss out if we adopt just one perspective and not the other.

In our present situation it is doubly important to use both languages. Neither the language of psychology nor the language of spirituality works for everyone. We live in a fragmented society in which different people look at things from different perspectives; we can no longer rely on a single way of understanding things and expect everyone to understand it.

There has been much interest recently in work on the interface of science and religion, and what I am advocating here is one example of that; but applied specifically to the journey inwards which is, at the same time, both a spiritual and a psychological journey. I am not suggesting that the two perspectives are identical, or that what we take to be spirituality is really nothing more than psychology. I take both perspectives seriously on their own terms. Each can shed light on some aspects of the journey more than others, which is why we need both.

It would be a mistake to think that there is just one perspective from psychology, or just one from spirituality. In fact there are many different approaches within each, and I draw on them freely, in an eclectic way. The richness and diversity of both psychology and spirituality further help to avoid missing important things.

In my view there is no incompatibility between the two perspectives. Most contemporary psychology simply ignores religion, and is neither for it nor against it. However, many branches of psychology can be applied to understand different aspects of spiritual or religious paths. Some psychologists have been against religion, most notably Sigmund Freud. However, I think that was just a case of his personal opinions influencing his professional work as a psychologist.

Some psychologists have been explicitly interested in making room for a spiritual perspective in psychology. The best umbrella term for that kind of psychology is 'transpersonal psychology', though that includes within it various different approaches. Perhaps the most important contribution of the spiritual perspective to understanding the inner journey is to leave space for more than the human individual.

The psychology of C.G. Jung is one that easily takes a spiritual perspective on board. In fact, much of his psychology could be seen as a translation into psychology of spiritual wisdom. For example, at the heart of his psychology is the 'Self', a kind of higher and complete self, which is also the image of God in the psyche. The journey of 'individuation', in which the Self becomes more of a reality, is both a psychological and a spiritual journey.

Perhaps the most important contribution of psychology to understanding the inner journey is to emphasise that it does not involve everyone conforming to the same template, but rather envisages that each person should realise their own distinctive potential. For many, Jesus plays an important role in this process. He is a model of someone who fulfilled his own potential and destiny, and is available as an inspiration and support for anyone who embarks on this journey of personal transformation for themselves. Being inspired by Jesus and becoming our true selves are not in tension with each other; they turn out to be just different aspects of the same process.

*Question:*

*What way of talking about your inner journey is most helpful for you, and why?*

## Heights and Depths

I want now to develop a fuller argument for why psychology and spirituality need each other when it comes to talking about the inner life.

Notice the different spatial metaphors that they characteristically use. Psychology often talks about going deep, especially with 'depth psychology'. Psychology wants to get to the bottom of things. Religion, in contrast, talks about raising up, or lifting up. At the heart of the Mass, the priest says, 'Lift up your hearts,' and the people reply, 'We lift them up to the Lord.' These seem to be in conflict. Religion is trying to go up and psychology is trying to go down. How can anyone do both?

Actually, I don't think there is ultimately any conflict here. If you go infinitely high and infinitely deep, you seem to end up in the same place, albeit by different routes. Either way, you end up at the ultimate spiritual reality that we call 'God'. It is similar to the way mathematicians say that parallel lines meet at infinity; or (another metaphor), 'all roads lead to Rome'.

There are pitfalls on the journey inwards, and it is easy to make mistakes. For example, someone's journey inwards can really be going rather well. But then they can start to feel pleased at how it is going and their pride spoils everything. It is easy to get so caught up in the journey inwards that you become blind to such traps. Keeping the perspectives of both psychology and spirituality in play reduces the risk of being oblivious to such pitfalls. Having two perspectives gives you a double chance of realising when you are going off track.

There are different hazards in a journey inwards that is entirely framed in terms of religion and ignores the psychological, and one that is entirely framed in terms of psychology and ignores the spiritual. Psychology without spirituality can become bogged down and lose direction and purpose; it can become so introspective that it becomes disconnected from anything around it. Psychology, left to itself, can drown in introspection and egocentricity. Raising your sights and taking a God's eye view of things for a moment can help you take your bearings and recover contact with what is beyond yourself.

There are very different hazards in spirituality without psychology, like the dangers of building on shallow or weak foundations. The resulting building is unstable and unable to withstand adverse conditions. It is easily blown about by fads and fancies and is particularly vulnerable to self-deception. Without psychology we can easily imagine (or pretend) that we are more spiritual than we actually are. The spiritual path, left to itself, is often tempted to take a shortcut that doesn't quite work and is really just papering over the cracks. It is like covering up unhappiness with what some psychologists call 'manic defence'.

My response to the dilemma of which language to use is to say that we need both. We need psychology to help us to go deep, and we need religion and spirituality to help us to lift our hearts and see the big picture. I believe there is no incompatibility, and that both psychology and religion are better when they have the humility to recognise that they benefit from the other. Then, as St Paul puts it, we can know the 'breadth and length and height and depth' of the love of God (Ephesians 3:18–19). Try emphasising the word 'and' in that quote. Making use of both psychology and religion can also bring us to greater heights and depths of self-knowledge.

> *Question:*
>
> *In your own inner journey, do you rely more*
> *on psychology or spirituality?*
> *How could you become more balanced?*

## Head and Heart

The journey inwards involves both head and heart, and the two need to work together. Humans, more than any other species, have two modes of cognition popularly known as 'head' and 'heart'. The fact that language is so much more developed in humans than in other species means that we can operate at the level of abstract thought more than any other species. But we have also retained the older (in evolutionary terms) capacity to function more intuitively, without pausing to articulate what we comprehend about our circumstances and what it is best to do.

There is a rough mapping of head on to left brain and of heart on to right brain. Ideas about the two sides of the brain were under a cloud for a while, but they have recently been rehabilitated in a long and brilliant book by Iain McGilchrist, *The Master and his Emissary*. As McGilchrist points out, if you are forced to choose between the two sides of the brain, it is the left brain, the co-called 'dominant' hemisphere, that you can more easily manage without. With just the right hemisphere, the more intuitive half of the brain, people can cope pretty well with the practical business of living, even if they don't have language. With just the left hemisphere, people can talk, but are so totally devoid of common sense that they simply can't cope with practical living.

The left hemisphere is physically very tightly interconnected and tends to live in its own little world. It tends to optimism and arrogance and assumes it can get everything sorted out. The right hemisphere is better connected to the physical body, relates better to people and to social context. It is more downbeat, more humble about what it doesn't know, more open to mystery, and has a stronger sense of the Other, beyond its own world. McGilchrist's view is that the right brain is better equipped to be the 'Master'; but the left brain, which is a useful 'emissary' or servant, has tended to be assertive and to take over as Master.

McGilchrist thinks this has been pretty disastrous. The second part of his book is a broad, sweeping account of Western intellectual history over the last few hundred years, which he sees as a story of the increasing dominance of the left hemisphere, albeit with some swings back in the other direction, like the Romantic Movement. He identifies various current symptoms of left-brain dominance, like the obsession with computer games and the rise in autistic spectrum disorders.

There are various things that might provide an escape route from this potentially disastrous trend in Western civilisation, like art and religion, but he sees both as having been hijacked by left-brain approaches. They ought to be able to help us to rebalance, and to lead us back to a greater reliance on intuitive wisdom and a greater sense of connectedness. However, in many places, religion and art have been so distorted by the dominance of the left brain that they can no longer do that.

Left-brain religion wants to get everything neatly tied down and specified. So, with religion, it wants to strip away the sense of mystery. It thinks it can know about God and know what a correct religious life consists of. But that is always a distortion of religion. Religion lends itself more naturally to a right-brain approach, with its natural sense of the Other, of connectedness and of humility. Dogmatic, literalist religion looks like a left brain takeover of religion. It has the arrogant precision associated with left-brain thinking.

The best way for humans to connect with God is through the heart. The head has its place in religious life but, when it comes to God, the knowing of the heart is the real thing. There are many witnesses I can call on to support me in this. One is that great Catholic of the nineteenth century, Cardinal Newman, whose motto was 'cor ad cor loquitur' (heart speaks unto heart). Another is that great mathematician and philosopher, Blaise Pascal, who describes the memorable occasion when he experienced the true God, the God of Abraham, Isaac and Jacob, not the God of the philosophers and the learned. It was an experience that gave him certitude, feeling, joy and peace.

If we are to talk about the deepest religious experiences (as Pascal and many others have tried to do), there is a sense that we are translating from the original wordless realm in which we felt connection with God to some other language or code that doesn't quite capture the experience. We can talk about it, yes, but in doing so we find we are offering a translation of the original experience, not quite the experience itself.

Even when words are used in religion, they are used differently from how they are used in many other areas of life. They are used rather poetically and with a rich network of associations. One very clear example is the idea of death followed by resurrection, associated with the death of Jesus. The same schema comes up in thinking about baptism, with the laying down of old life and taking up a new one. It comes up again in the experience of rebuilding one's life after some big loss or personal disaster. Language that captures such a network of associations is thick and rich.

It sometimes comes up in public events. The bombing of the cathedral in Coventry and its subsequent rebuilding was explicitly seen in these terms. There was a German bombing raid on Coventry in November 1940 and the cathedral caught fire. They tried to put the fire out, but their efforts failed and they had to retreat and watch it burn. As they watched, the Provost, Dick Howard, had a powerful religious experience. He felt that the cathedral belonged to Christ, not to them; it was the body of Christ that was burning there; Christ was being put to death all over again. However, when Christ is put to death he always rises again, and he felt that the cathedral would rise again, because it belonged to Christ. There was a striking collapse of the difference in time and space between the crucifixion of Jesus on

Golgotha and the burning of Coventry Cathedral. In Dick Howard's mind (or heart) they became virtually the same event. It was a kind of déjà vu experience: 'I've been here before.'

The story of Coventry Cathedral has moved me deeply, as I grew up in war-damaged Coventry and saw a new cathedral being built. The Coventry story is one to which I will return several times in this book.

> *Question:*
> *Can you sense within yourself the difference between thinking*
> *about God with your head and responding to him*
> *with your heart?*

## Towards Integration

Spiritual paths have several different facets. They involve what people think, do and feel. Ideas, practices and experiences are all involved. When mistakes are made in how the spiritual life is pursued, tensions are set up between these different facets. When it goes well, these different aspects of personality become increasingly integrated.

One of the striking features of the personal transformation that the spiritual life offers is that the various facets of the spiritual life come into harmony with one another. Thoughts, emotions and actions are aligned and work together harmoniously. Each one supports the others in fruitful mutual reinforcement, without tension or strain. Every element in someone's personality works together in a harmonious and balanced way.

A way of functioning develops that is fulfilling for the individual, and which engages creatively and effectively with what is going on around. The person becomes aligned with whatever is good, true and beautiful. In religious shorthand we might say that it involves our becoming the people God called us to be.

Imagine some iron filings scattered on a sheet of paper; they are disorganised and pointing in many different directions. When a magnet is introduced, the filings quickly organise themselves in a pattern and become co-ordinated. When the spiritual life goes well it produces something similar to that kind of co-ordination. The various elements of a personality start to work together around a spiritual centre. In the psychology of C.G. Jung, the name for that spiritual centre is the 'Self'.

It is useful to distinguish between true and false forms of spiritual transformation. In less satisfactory forms of spiritual transformation, there can be uncomfortable struggles between different parts of the personality. That produces an unstable and often unconvincing attempt at spirituality.

A common problem is that people try too hard to produce the appearance of a deeply spiritual life, but in a way that lacks deep roots and is inherently unstable. An appearance of spiritual depth can be created by trying to control other aspects of personality rather than by transforming them. However, whatever part of the personality has been sidelined can start to reassert itself.

Jesus' story about seed being sown in different kinds of soil is very apposite here (Mark 1–9). Some approaches to the spiritual life are like seed sown on shallow soil with no deep roots. Also relevant is Jesus' conversation with the Samaritan woman in which he promises that the water he will give her will be a 'spring of water gushing up to eternal life' (John 4:14). A deep spirituality is like that inner spring welling up from within.

It is a tricky matter how much self-discipline is helpful in the spiritual life. There is certainly a place for it and we need some disciplined regularity in our spiritual practice. However, being too organised and disciplined about it can lead us astray. In the end we find that we cannot turn ourselves into holy people, but there is a way of opening ourselves to something above and beyond us that will transform us. I like St Augustine's dictum, 'Love God and do what you will'. If our hearts connect with God, and we are coming from the right place, then things start to work out well.

We might draw an analogy with how people play sport. Sometimes people talk about the 'natural' game of tennis, basketball or whatever, in which people surrender themselves and let the game play itself through them, rather than trying too hard to play well. It is very similar to the spiritual experience of 'grace' that is beyond yourself.

You may need to practise hard at tennis, and get pretty good at it, before you can surrender to the game and let the game play itself through you. In the same way, you may need to put time and effort into the spiritual life before you can surrender yourself fully to grace and let grace and spirituality flow through you. But in the end, things work much better, in a way that is more satisfying and more convincing, if you can make the switch to doing things that way.

People sometimes talk about letting prayer flow through them, rather than trying very hard to pray. That is similar to a tennis player playing the natural game of tennis. I think that is what St Paul is referring to when he says 'we do not know how to pray as we ought, but that very Spirit intercedes with sighs too deep for words' (Romans 8:26). Prayer is bigger than any one of us. There is a stream of prayer in which we can participate as and when we are able; it is not down to us to do it all.

To come back to where I started this chapter, it is one of the benefits of looking at the inner journey from the perspective of psychology as well as spirituality that it is easier to spot when shallow roots are leading to an imitation of the real thing. If the inner life looks convincing from the perspectives of *both* psychology *and* spirituality it is more likely to be authentic and transformative.

*Question:*

*Have there been moments in your spiritual life when it felt natural to just let your spiritual life happen rather than having to work at it?*

## Bible Study

Read Jesus' story of the sower who sows seed on different kinds of ground (Mark 4:1–9), and explore that as a metaphor for different ways of going about the spiritual journey. How can you approach your own spiritual life in a way that will be like sowing seed in good soil?

Look also at the story of Jesus and the Samaritan woman (John 4:7–15), and take that as another metaphor for the spiritual life. What kind of spiritual life would be like that inner spring, 'gushing up to eternal life'?

Look also at what St Paul says about the Spirit praying within us in Romans 8:26–27.

## Background and Sources

A useful guide to the psychology of spirituality is Larry Culliford (2010) *The Psychology of Spirituality: An Introduction.* Jessica Kingsley Publishers. See also Fraser Watts (2017) *Psychology, Religion and Spirituality.* Cambridge University Press (especially chapter eight on spirituality).

For a classic guide to the journey inwards from the perspective of spiritual practice, see F. C. Happold (1968) *Journey Inwards*. Darton, Longman & Todd.

For a comparable book from the perspective of Jungian psychology see Christopher Bryant (1987) *Journey to the Centre: Explorations in the Realm of the Spirit*. Darton, Longman & Todd.

On heights and depths see the paper on 'peaks and vales' in James Hillman (1979) *Puer Papers*. Spring Publications. On head and heart, see Fraser Watts and Geoff Dumbreck (eds.) *Head and Heart: Perspectives from Religion and Psychology*. John Templeton Press.

I have been much influenced by Stephen Verney's (1995) *Water into Wine: An Introduction to St John's Gospel*. Darton, Longman & Todd. Chapter four on Jesus and the Samaritan woman is especially relevant to the suggested Bible study.

There is a helpful mapping between psychological and theological approaches to personality in Peter Morea (1997) *In Search of Personality: Christians and Modern Psychology*. SCM Press.

# Section One
*Personal Issues*

# Chapter Two:
## *Coping with Stress*

### Recognising Stress

Most people's lives are stressful. The Psalms are full of cries from the heart from people who feel beleaguered, under more pressure than they can bear, and are the butt of people's derision and hostility. Look at Psalm 56 for example:

'Be gracious to me, O God, for people trample on me; all day long foes oppress me; my enemies trample on me all day long, for many fight against me. . . All day long they seek to injure my cause; all their thoughts are against me for evil. They stir up strife, they lurk, they watch my steps' (Psalm 56:1–2 and 5–6).

Stress is not all bad. It can challenge us and bring out the best in us. People often perform better with moderate stress. However, there is a limit to how much stress anyone can cope with. When stress rises beyond what we can handle, it brings out the worst in us.

A key part of wisdom in managing stress is to keep an eye on how much stress you are under. Try to keep it within the middle range, neither so little that you become lazy, bored or complacent, but not so much that you start to fall apart. We generally have some degree of control over how much stress we are under. There are some stresses over which we have little control, but we can try to avoid being too overstretched for too long.

Stress shows itself in various ways. Many people have an area where stress shows itself first. It may be that you sleep badly, get irritable, get headaches, get stomach trouble, get backache, or whatever. Our bodies are often helpful here, and they have their own wisdom. If we pay attention to what our bodies are telling us about how stressed we are, it will help us to keep stress levels down to what we can cope with. Take a moment to think what your warning signs are that you are getting overstressed.

Change can be stressful in itself. Even changes that we may really want, like getting married, involve a lot of fresh challenges, and can be stressful. Much depends on what other changes are going on at the same time. If one area of our lives is stressful, it helps if other areas are relatively stable. We can't easily cope with too many things changing at once.

It is also stressful to have too much going on, being pulled in too many different directions, so we don't know what we ought to be concentrating on. If our energies become too fragmented, we can no longer do anything properly. However, people differ on this, and some people cope pretty well with multitasking.

Every situation we find ourselves in has its own particular pattern of stresses.

There are particular stresses associated with work roles. The expectations can be rather diffuse and unmanageable, leaving people feeling that they don't really know what is wanted of them. Alternatively, expectations can be over-specific, leaving people feeling that they have no scope to shape their work for themselves.

Being a parent is often quite stressful, despite the satisfactions it may also bring, and it can sometimes seem that there is no way to get it right. There are particular stresses attached to the caring professions, including being a religious pastor. People seem to have particularly unrealistic expectations of pastors. Their opinions of them also often go to extremes; people tend to either idealise them or to be very critical of them. That can be very confusing.

It is also stressful to be faced with problems that we don't know how to tackle; or with challenges that seem completely beyond us; or to have to tackle problems alone that we might be able to tackle with other people, but not single-handed.

*Question:*
*What are the biggest stresses for you at the moment?*
*Notice what signs of stress you are showing now.*

## Ways of Coping

Stress partly depends on our perceptions, which gives us a bit of leverage. We may have unrealistic expectations of our job, our church, our family, and we sometimes resist perceiving them realistically, increasing our stress through our resistance.

We can exaggerate how difficult challenges are, in a way that makes them even harder to handle than they would have been otherwise. If we have had similar difficulties before, that may add an even more negative cast to our present problems.

Equally, we can underestimate stresses, in a way that leads us to think we can handle things that we actually can't. It helps in stress management to see challenges straight, without exaggeration or minimisation.

Stress also depends on what resources we think we have, and whether we think we will be able to cope. We all seem to find it very hard to read ourselves right. We either slide into underestimating ourselves, or we take on more than we can manage in a way that is heroic but unrealistic. It helps in coping with stress to see ourselves as we really are, knowing our strengths, but not exaggerating them. It may help in that to learn to see ourselves as God would see us.

It is natural for us to become more alert when we are facing challenges; that helps us to respond to stress effectively. However, it is really important to be able to switch off when the challenge is over. The key problem with people who get overstressed is not that they rise to a challenge, but that they can't switch off when the challenge is over.

There should be a natural ebb and flow in how aroused we are, like the ebb and flow of the tides. There are times when the tide needs to come in, reaching a high-water point of alertness. But the tide needs to go out again when the emergency is over. That doesn't always happen.

There are various things we can do to improve our ability to cope with stress.

We can enhance our ability to cope with stress by managing how we think. If we think too much about how desperate things are, we undermine our ability to cope. But it doesn't help to go to the other extreme, and to try to pretend we have no problems; that is just unconvincing. The most helpful approach is a 'coping' stance, recognising that we have problems, but trusting that we will be able to cope with them.

Looking after our bodies can also be helpful. That includes giving ourselves time for rest and relaxation, for burning off the effects of stress through exercise, and allowing ourselves plenty of sleep. Most people benefit from some way of doing physical relaxation. There are many approaches; just find one that works for you.

Just being quiet in the presence of God when a challenge has passed is a good way of winding down. As we make more use of quiet prayer time, we will realise how helpful it is, and may come to depend on it. When Jesus became overstretched by the numbers of people seeking healing, he went away for some quiet prayer time to renew himself. It is a good example for us to follow.

> *Question:*
> *Which ways of coping with stress work best for you?*

## Support from Others

How stressful things become also depends on how much we feel we can count on others. When there are people we can turn to for help, things seem less stressful. We are social beings – we are not meant to 'go it alone'.

The more we can build up networks of mutual support, the better we will all be able to cope. If we support other people when they need us, they are more likely to help us when we need it ourselves. Try to steer a middle path in how much help you ask for. Don't ask for so much help that it scares people off, but don't be afraid to ask for any help at all.

Different people help in different ways. Some people may help us cope in every possible way, but it is common to get different kinds of help from different people. Some people may help us emotionally; others more practically. Some people may help us with quite small things, but very immediately. Others may help in bigger ways, but it may take longer to arrange that.

Religious life can help in coping with stress. Trusting that we can cope depends on what resources we think we have available; for religious people, trusting in God is perhaps the most important part of that. Religious coping works best if we feel that God is working with us to help us get through. That works better than feeling that God expects us to stand on our own feet; it is also better than feeling that we can leave everything to God, and that nothing is expected of us.

For religious people, trust in God is not about avoiding the hard times. Rather, in the light of our own and others' life experiences, we have *grounds* for trust that God will once again bring us through. It is generally best not to be over-specific in exactly how God should act to help and support us; better just to be confident that he will, even if the form that support takes sometimes surprises us. Trust in God is deep and far-reaching. These words from Isaiah convey in a marvellously reassuring way what God can do for us:

> I have called you by name, you are mine. When you pass through the waters, I will be with you; and through the rivers, they shall not overwhelm you; when you walk through fire you shall not be burned, and the flame shall not consume you . . . you are precious in my sight, and honoured, and I love you . . . Do not fear, for I am with you (Isaiah 43:1–5).

Imagine those verses as vividly as you can – imagine God present with you in the burning flames or torrents of water. Or imagine God walking beside you in whatever difficult situation you find yourself – imagine it in as much detail as you can, using all your senses: smell, sight, hearing, touch. Be open to God's guidance – to his plan to bring you through. Be open to that deep, hidden wisdom and energy (whatever you call it) that can guide you through difficult times in your life.

Some Christians have a vivid sense of how angels can guide and support them in times of danger and difficulty, perhaps through a dream. For example, when the life of the infant Jesus was in danger from Herod, an angel appeared to Joseph to urge him to take Jesus to Egypt (Matthew 2:13). Later, when Herod died, an angel told him it was safe to return (Matthew 2:19–20). You may have had an experience yourself of an angel guiding you out of danger, or you may know someone who has. Jesus himself was supported by angels at key moments, such as in his temptation in the wilderness.

Sometimes Christians also feel the guidance and support of saintly people (or even quite ordinary people) who have passed on into the nearer presence of God. Some people feel that they can be helped to cope with difficult situations by people we have been close to but who have passed on. Our memory of them can help us, of course, but sometimes people feel that the departed are still present beside us, in a quite specific way.

> *Question:*
> *What kinds of support have been most helpful to you?*

## Worry

Anxiety is part of the stuff of life for all of us. We are beset with so many problems at so many levels, ranging from our purely private concerns, through many layers of interaction with others, to concerns about the sustainability of the planet. Unless we close ourselves off entirely from noticing what is going on, it is hard to see that we can avoid worry entirely.

Some people worry more than others. For some people, worry is quite circumscribed, whereas others worry about everything. Some people worry only from time to time; others worry all the time. Worry is not all bad; if we never worried we would not be prodded into action when we need to be, but worry can become excessive. Excessive worry can certainly be debilitating and make it difficult to get anything done. What is to be done about excessive worry?

Worry is perhaps the mental health problem about which the Bible has most to say. Jesus, in the Sermon on the Mount, tells people not to worry, or not to be anxious (translations differ). It is one of the longer passages in Jesus' teaching. Here it is:

> Therefore I tell you, do not worry about your life, what you will eat or what you will drink, or about your body, what you will wear. Is not life more than food, and the body more than clothing? Look at the birds of the air; they neither sow nor reap nor gather into barns, and yet your heavenly Father feeds them. Are you not of more value than they? And can any of you by worrying add a single hour to your span of life? And why do you worry about clothing? Consider the lilies of

the field, how they grow; they neither toil nor spin, yet I tell you, even Solomon in all his glory was not clothed like one of these. But if God so clothes the grass of the field, which is alive today and tomorrow is thrown into the oven, will he not much more clothe you – you of little faith? Therefore do not worry, saying, 'What will we eat?' or 'What will we drink?' or 'What will we wear?' For it is the Gentiles who strive for all these things; and indeed your heavenly Father knows that you need all these things. But strive first for the kingdom of God and his righteousness, and all these things will be given to you as well. So do not worry about tomorrow, for tomorrow will bring worries of its own. Today's trouble is enough for today (Matthew. 6:25–34).

There are several strands here. One is an encouragement to be focused on the present moment, rather than thinking too much about the future. It seems unlikely that Jesus meant that we should never think about the future, but at least we should not get so taken up with worry about the future that we cannot focus properly on what is happening right now. Focusing on the present enables us to deal with it better. It may also help to calm us to focus on what we need to do now rather than worrying about the future. If we get really engrossed in what we are doing we can have what has sometimes been called a 'flow' experience in which we are totally focused and we leave worry behind.

There is also a strand about priorities in what Jesus says. He is pointing out that many of the things we tend to worry about may not, on reflection, be as important as we think they are. Clothes are an interesting example. In prosperous Western society we can spend a lot of time on clothes. Jesus seems to be suggesting that, when you stop and think about it, many of the things we get concerned about, such as clothes, may not be as important as we assumed. Readjusting our priorities can help us to worry less.

There is another strand about trust and co-operation. We live in a society that is much more individualistic than that of Jesus. The background assumption seems to be that if any problems are to get fixed we will have to fix them ourselves; we can't depend on anyone else to do so. That is highly individualistic and, I suggest, unrealistic; we can't actually fix anything much entirely on our own.

Problems get fixed through co-operation, not by isolated individuals. Overcoming worry depends on recognising this, and learning to be more trusting.

There may be a close link between what Jesus says about worry and about prayer. The Lord's Prayer comes just a bit earlier in the same chapter, with the petition, 'Give us this day our daily bread.' Jesus urges people not to worry about what they will eat. It seems that worry and prayer are being presented as alternatives, and that Jesus is urging us to pray rather than worry, or to turn our worry into prayer.

> *Question:*
>
> *Reflect on some of the things that have helped you not to get eaten up with worry, and think whether you could use them more.*

## Prayer and Coping

Prayer is one of the ways in which people cope with stressful events. There are many different ways of praying, and no single right way. One kind of prayer that many people find helpful involves reflecting on past and future events in the presence of God. That is particularly helpful if there are stressful things going on in our lives.

One useful thing you can do, as you look back over recent events, is to cultivate gratitude. Psychological research has shown how helpful gratitude is. There is evidence to show that if you spend just five minutes a day keeping a log of things you are grateful for, it will improve your health, relationships, emotions, personality and career.

You don't need to be religious to benefit from practising gratitude, but religious people have a particular way of doing it that they call 'thanksgiving'. If you believe in God, you have someone to be grateful to, which may be easier than being grateful to no one in particular. Some Christians learn to be grateful for a very broad range of things. St Paul encourages us to 'give thanks in all circumstances' (1 Thessalonians 5:18). At first, that seems very puzzling. How can you be thankful for something painful in your life? But if you work at it, it changes the usual way in which we divide experiences up into those we like and those we don't like.

Learning to give thanks for everything leads us to look at how even very unwelcome things can help us to grow and develop, and can in the long run help us to fulfil our potential and set forward God's loving purposes for us. Thanksgiving can really help us to cope with the most difficult things.

In prayer, Christians often look at what they have done wrong, so as to 'confess' it. It may seem as though that is just going to make you feel very guilty, and be really unhelpful psychologically. However, it may actually turn out to be rather helpful. The point of confession is that it is followed by forgiveness; the intention is to release people from the sense of guilt, not to entrench them in it.

The other helpful aspect of confession, as far as coping is concerned, is that it can raise consciousness about how we contribute to things going wrong, for ourselves and for others. If confession makes us more aware of that, and helps us to draw back from things that are potentially damaging, it will have done a useful job, and made life easier to cope with.

Other parts of prayer look to the future. We all have hopes and fears about the future, and Christians often ask God for what they feel they most desire and need. Prayer can help us to discover what would *really* be in our best interests; we may then want to ask for that, rather than just for what we most desire.

There is deep religious wisdom about how God sometimes answers prayer in ways that are different from what we want or expect, but which may nevertheless be in our best interests. That leads us to reframe setbacks in our lives as ways that God may be answering prayer in our best interests. The more we can make sense of things, the better we will cope with them.

There has recently been much interest in how meditational spiritual practices such as mindfulness can help people cope. Mindfulness makes an important distinction between our core basic experiences and all the other judgements and reflections we build around them. One way of dealing with that would be to reframe maladaptive patterns of appraisal, but mindfulness trains people, rather, just to stay with basic experiences and not to go into the realms of more discursive and judgemental thinking at all. That seems to be a useful skill to acquire, though there is still some debate about just how helpful mindfulness actually is.

Some Christians have been concerned that mindfulness comes from an alien spiritual tradition. However, within Christianity, there is a broad range of spiritual practices, including some that are very much like mindfulness. However, for those who prefer, there are similar ways of meditating that are more explicitly Christian, and which are probably just as helpful.

Christians have often also used forms of breathing prayer, such as the Jesus Prayer, that are quite similar to other spiritual practices that involve a focus on breathing. In the Jesus Prayer, you breathe in, you say (or think) 'Lord Jesus Christ, Son of God,' and then, as you breathe out, 'have mercy on me, a sinner.' That repeated prayer becomes integrated with your breathing so, just as you are sustained physically by your breathing, you are sustained spiritually by this prayer.

> *Question:*
> *Think back over any times when prayer has helped you*
> *to get through.*

## Bible Study

The Old Testament story of Joseph includes a busy and stressful time for Joseph in Egypt (Genesis 41:33–52). See Sara Savage (2011) *Joseph: Insights for the Spiritual Journey.* SPCK. Chapter three.

Several of the Psalms speak quite powerfully about stress. I quoted Psalm 56 above. You could also look at Psalm 62:3–8 and Psalm 120. A great many Psalms convey the experience of desolation or persecution quite powerfully.

I quoted about what Jesus says about worry (Matthew 6:25–34). There is a similar passage in Luke 12:22–32. St Paul also echoes this teaching of Jesus: 'Do not worry about anything, but in everything by prayer and supplication with thanksgiving let your requests be made known to God' (Philippians 4:6). Think through the implications of the mindset Jesus is recommending.

When we are stressed it is tempting to become very judgemental about others, or to want to blame someone. Jesus generally seems to want to avoid that. For example, in John's Gospel, he wants to avoid condemning the woman caught in adultery (John 8:1–11). In the story of the blind man who receives his sight back, he rejects the question of who is to blame for his being born blind (John 9:2–3).

There is an important strand running through the Bible about taking rest, which can be important in coping. The Sabbath is a day of rest, and Christians are encouraged to enter into that rest

(Hebrews 4:9–11). There is a similar strand about the importance of withdrawing from the demands of life for prayer, and that is a feature of how Jesus lives his life (e.g. Mark 1:35; 6:46; 14:32).

## Background and Sources

The book that set the stage for current psychological thinking about stress and coping is Richard Lazarus and Susan Folkman (1984/2000) *Stress, Appraisal and Coping*. Springer Publishing. They emphasise how dependent stress is on our assessment of the demands being made on us, and of our ability to cope with them; it is primarily a cognitive approach to stress and coping. The last fifty years have seen elaborations and applications of that basic approach, but no fundamental changes. A comprehensive source book of recent research is Susan Folkman (ed.) (2010) *The Oxford Handbook of Stress, Health, and Coping*. New York: Oxford University Press.

An excellent book from that early period of work on stress and coping with a more applied focus is Donald Meichenbaum (1983) *Coping with Stress*. Century. There are many comparable more recent books, such as Jane Plant and Janet Stephenson (2008) *Beating Stress, Anxiety and Depression*. Piatkus Books.

Religion provides an important context for coping. The classic source on this is Kenneth Pargament (1997) *The Psychology of Religion and Coping: Theory, Research, Practice*. New York: Guilford Press. There is useful material in Fraser Watts, Rebecca Nye and Sara Savage (2002) *Psychology for Christian Ministry*. Routledge (see pp. 9–15 on prayer and pp. 251–57 on stress in clergy).

On gratitude see Robert Emmons (2013) *Gratitude Works! a 21-Day Program for Creating Emotional Prosperity*. Jossey Bass. A good introduction to mindfulness is Mark Williams and Danny Penman (2010) *Mindfulness: A Practical Guide to Finding Peace in a Frantic World*. Piatkus. For a Christian perspective on mindfulness see Joanna Collicutt, Roger Bretherton and Jennifer Brickman (2016) *Being Mindful, Being Christian: An Invitation to Mindful Discipleship*. Monarch Books.

There are some helpful chapters in Russell Re Manning (ed.) (2018) *Mutual Enrichment Between Theology, Psychology and Religious Life*. Routledge. I am indebted here to the chapter on 'Worry and Prayer' by Chris Cook. There are also contrasting chapters on mindfulness, with Mark Williams taking a positive view, and Miguel Farias being more sceptical.

# Chapter Three
## *Depression*

## Experiencing Depression

I want to focus now on depression. It is both a very common mental health problem, and also one where many different factors intersect. Biological, social, developmental and spiritual factors all come together in depression, more than with any other mental health problem. I want to recognise the importance of all these aspects, in an even-handed way, rather than saying that one aspect of depression is fundamental and all the others are secondary.

Many aspects of depression raise interesting issues from a Christian point of view. I want here to look particularly at the depressive mindset, which is so negative. I will also look at the role of good levels of social support, which can be critical; and at how we react to our own depression, which plays a significant role in determining whether or not it spirals out of control.

We all have some experience of depression, so I suggest you take a moment to connect with what it feels like, and take an insider's perspective, not just think about it in abstract, looking at it from the outside, so to speak. When we are depressed we can feel so guilty that we keep on beating ourselves up;

or so ashamed that we can't face meeting anyone;

or so angry that we want to punch the world in the face;

or so lacking in hope that we have no energy to do anything.

Sometimes we feel as though we have lost everything important, or feel that we are a complete failure.

The Psalms contain some vivid accounts of depression, like this one:

> My days pass away like smoke, and my bones burn like a furnace.
> My heart is stricken and withered like grass; I am too wasted to eat my bread.
> Because of my loud groaning my bones cling to my skin.
> I am like an owl of the wilderness, like a little owl of the waste places.
> I lie awake; I am like a lonely bird on the housetop (Psalm 102:3-7).

The poets have also given us vivid accounts of depression, like the nineteenth-century priest-poet Gerard Manley Hopkins, who knew what it was like to greet the dawn after a tortured, sleepless night: 'I wake and feel the fell of dark, not day. What hours, O what black hours we have spent This night!'

At the outset, let us take three key points on board about depression.

Firstly, a crucial aspect of depression is how we react to it. It is easy to get upset about being depressed; there is also a second-order depression, where you are depressed about being depressed. That plays a key role in keeping depression going. We make depression worse by telling ourselves how intolerable it is. We live in a world in which people expect 'happiness' as the everyday norm. Depression really is bad; there is no denying that, and we should work to free ourselves from its grip. But, if we bear depression patiently, letting go of the fantasy of a perfectly happy life, it will do less damage.

I suspect that over the last hundred years or so, people have become more intolerant of feeling unhappy; we now expect to feel good all the time. That has led us to put a lot of effort into developing therapy for depression, which can certainly be helpful. However, I think there is a danger that our modern dislike of depression may actually make us more vulnerable to it. It means that a few days of sadness can be so upsetting that it can spiral out of control into depression.

Secondly, depression raises difficult issues about whether we are to blame for being depressed; blaming ourselves for it makes it worse. At the other end of the spectrum we may feel helpless under its dead weight, unable to find a path out of that; that experience of helplessness also makes it worse. We need to find a path between blame on the one hand and the feeling of helplessness on the other.

Depression can be brought on by difficult circumstances such as loss, betrayal, disappointed hopes, the unfairness of life. However, we aren't completely helpless in depression, because we sometimes contribute to it ourselves, or keep ourselves locked in it, by how we think and the way we lead our lives. We are usually neither entirely responsible for our depression, nor completely unable to do anything to help ourselves. We can't just snap out of depression, but we can take sensible steps towards leaving it behind.

Finally, depression is never a punishment from God. God could never wish depression on us. Using religion to point a finger of blame at people for being depressed (or at ourselves) is a misuse of belief in a loving God, and impedes the flow of his loving kindness. Nevertheless, if we take depression as a challenge that helps us to grow and develop, some good may come out of it. As the Psalms say: 'Happy are those who, going through the vale of misery, use it for a well, and the pools are filled with water (Psalm 84:6).

> *Question:*
> *Do you sometimes respond to your low periods in ways*
> *that make them worse?*

## Negative Thinking

Depression colours how we think. When we slide into depression we start to think very negatively about everything. That sets up a vicious circle and our negative thinking does more than anything else to keep us locked in depression. This is important, from a practical point of view, because it gives us a place where we can get some leverage over our depression and weaken its grip on us.

The first step is to be more aware of our negative thinking. It is often so familiar that we hardly notice it. It fades into the background so it can creep around in our minds, doing its destructive work, almost without our realising. So, the first step is to become more aware of our negative thinking. It is often extremely repetitive, like a short section of tape that keeps on playing, over and over. There are usually three strands in this negative thinking:

*Ourselves*: we feel we are worthless and useless, incapable of doing any good or getting anything right.

*The World*: We feel that everyone is against us and that no one really cares about us; that life has repeatedly kicked us in the teeth.

*The Future*: We feel there is no future for us at all, or not one worth having; the future seems hopeless, black and empty.

It is not just having these negative ideas that drags us down, it is also *how* we think these thoughts. We can think them in ways that are so black and white, so absolute, so unwilling to be the slightest bit generous to ourselves. A little unhappy moment becomes exaggerated into something completely catastrophic.

Once you become aware of this repetitive tape of negative thoughts, it helps to make a big effort to turn it off. Each time you notice your negative thoughts, just turn the tape off. It will start up again, of course; but each time just turn it off again. Don't get frustrated or disappointed; just calmly, patiently and firmly keep on turning it off. At first it is difficult, but you will find you quickly get better at it. That is the essence of the cognitive therapy approach to depression, though anyone planning to use it would be well advised to get more detailed guidance. It is not a panacea for all forms of depression, but it has helped many people and there is a solid body of evidence supporting its usefulness.

There is also a distinctive pattern of 'attributions' in depression, seen in how we explain the good and bad things that happen to us, i.e. what we put them down to. If you are depressed, you see yourself as responsible for the bad things that happen to you; and see bad things as resulting from qualities that mess up everything, not just one or two specific things; and qualities that will never change. In contrast, good things are attributed to external factors that can't be depended on, such as pure luck. That accentuates bad experiences and dismisses positive ones. It is something else that is addressed in cognitive therapy.

Underneath negative thinking there are often genuine life problems. But notice how negative thinking exaggerates everything and over-generalises from it. You may have messed up some particular thing, but don't let that turn into the idea that you can't do anything right. You may feel low, but learn to just attend to how you actually feel without building a huge 'castle in the air' of negative interpretations on top of it.

The negative thinking that is characteristic of depression is not at all where faith leads; hope is fundamental to the Christian mindset.

However, faith does not necessarily lead to the opposite of negative thinking either. It doesn't lead us to think that everything is OK or to be always optimistic. Faith leads neither to the kind of excessively negative thinking that saps motivation, nor to the kind of rosy optimism that doesn't recognise the reality of problems and difficulties.

There is an intriguing phenomenon known as 'depressive realism'. In some situations it seems that the judgements of depressed people are more accurate than those of people who are not depressed. Though the evidence for this is admittedly somewhat mixed, I suspect there is something in it. People with a depressive outlook sometimes believe they are seeing things accurately, without a distorting rosy glow, and see that as a kind of virtue.

Many of us go through life, looking at ourselves through somewhat rose-tinted spectacles. Depression strips all that away. There is often a harsh realism in depression; it leads us to see ourselves more as others see us. But, when we come to recognise our faults more clearly, it is important not to be overwhelmed by them and not to think that we are altogether useless.

I suggest that spirituality leads to a commitment to balance and objectivity, rather than to an unremittingly positive outlook. We need a balance between the negative thinking characteristic of depression and the over-positive thinking that is often an alternative to it, what some might call a 'manic defence'. Something similar emerges from research on coping styles. Negativity doesn't help people to cope, but neither does it help to pretend there are no problems and challenges. The most helpful stance is to recognise problems but to believe you will be able to handle them.

It is actually quite hard to be objective in our perceptions of other people. We tend to view other people more favourably or less favourably than we should, and that is driven by our own needs. Similarly we see other people as more or less needy than they are, for our own reasons. A balanced and accurate stance is probably even harder to achieve with ourselves than with other people. The pull towards either over-negative or over-positive self-evaluations is very strong. It is remarkably difficult to learn to see ourselves accurately, but it is an important spiritual virtue.

> *Question:*
> *Can you spot when you are thinking negatively,*
> *and can you turn it off?*

# Towards Hope

A spiritual life does not lead either to optimism or pessimism; it avoids both. It tries to take a balanced view. There is good and bad around, forces working in both directions. It is unwise to close your eyes to either.

However, a spiritual life *does* lead to hope. Hope is very different from optimism. Hope does not depend on circumstances being favourable; indeed it can come into its own when circumstances are very unfavourable. There were people who managed to keep hope alive even in Nazi concentration camps.

Hope is much more flexible and versatile than optimism. It is a general attitude rather than a prediction about what is going to happen. It also carries a commitment to work for a better future. Optimism is rather passive; it just takes stock and predicts what is going to happen. Hope, in contrast, sets about transforming the future.

Depressed people are often rather pessimistic, but I suggest that it is a lack of hope rather than a lack of optimism that is really debilitating. It is almost impossible to be optimistic when you are depressed. However, if you have deep-seated hope, it will encourage you to transform the present blackness into something better.

Hope is not just expecting things to go well; it has deep roots. The well-known psychologist Erik Erikson proposed a theory of psycho-social development in which the basic virtue of the first stage (up to about one and a half years) is hope, and revolved around issues of trust and distrust. If we can continue to be hopeful in difficult times, we are digging deep in our personal development.

Hope also arises from deep convictions and a positive, trusting attitude to the future. For Christians, it arises from faith in God and, as St Paul puts it, in 'things unseen' (Romans 8:24). Hope that is grounded in faith is powerful and can triumph over depression. If we have a strong sense that nothing will be able 'to separate us from the love of God in Christ Jesus our Lord' (Romans 8:39), that will be enormously helpful.

It is basic Christian work to clear away the clouds of overly negative thinking so that some shafts of hope can shine through. Whenever we turn despair into hope we find that we are connecting with God, because that is what God does. It echoes how Jesus' crucifixion led on to Resurrection. Take the well-known prayer attributed to St Francis and apply it to yourself: 'Where there is despair, let me bring hope; where there is darkness, let me bring light; and where there is sadness, let me bring joy.' We can bring this help to ourselves, as well as to others, by tackling our negative thinking. Hope can rise up from our despair.

We humans have a remarkable capacity for thinking and planning, for weighing things up, for constantly evaluating ourselves and others. In depression, all that takes a negative turn and gets out of hand. It is a way of thinking which leads us to be either optimistic or pessimistic and, if we are depressed and faced with that choice, we are always bound to go towards pessimism.

Of course, our basic pessimistic instincts can be challenged. We can employ our rational minds to help make the case that our pessimistic instincts are exaggerated, and that things are not as bad we thought. But there is also a path of hope which is less rationally based and which digs deeper into our own past, and into faith in God (or providence).

Finding the path out of depression often involves drawing back from excessive judgementalism, from endlessly deciding what we approve of and what we don't, and reverting to basic hope and trust. Being too judgemental is something Jesus warns us against in the Sermon on the Mount: 'Do not judge, so that you may not be judged' (Matthew 7:1–3).

> *Question:*
> *What resources can you find within you or beyond you to keep hope alive in difficult times?*

## Getting Help

Depression is also intertwined with our circumstances and relationships. Our relationships can contribute to depression, but they can also help to lift us out of it.

Sometimes there are difficult life events that precipitate depression. Such events are most likely to make us depressed if they are similar to other events we have found it hard to cope with in the past. Then they can quickly take us back into a bad place where we have been before and drag us down.

But it makes a big difference whether we have good personal support. We are less likely to get depressed when something challenging happens if we feel well supported by someone close to us. Such support is equally important in getting through depression.

For most people the key thing is to have someone we trust, whom we see regularly, who understands us, wants the best for us and in whom we can confide. In other words, we need someone who shows us authentic love; nothing is more powerful in warding off depression. To stay clear of depression, most of us need such a confidante ourselves, and we also may be able to play that role for others.

Sometimes we are not open to people giving us the support we need. We may be distrustful, unwilling to open up, or too proud to admit that we are not quite coping. Sometimes, after putting off asking for help for too long, we go to the other extreme and ask for so much help that people get scared by the depth of our neediness and 'run a mile'. It is best if we seek support regularly, but in moderation. And things quickly go wrong if we try to manipulate people into giving us the support we need, rather than letting them give it freely.

When we are depressed we tend to hide away, and not go anywhere or do anything. That is an understandable reaction to depression, but it cuts us off from the things that could help us, and so keeps depression going. If we can gradually manage to get back to functioning as though we were not depressed, it builds up our confidence and sense of fulfilment, and helps us to shake off depression.

For Christians, there is an extra source of support available in God. If we have a strong sense of the unseen, loving presence of God, we will feel better supported. Because support is so important in warding off depression, or helping us to find a way out of it, a strong sense of the unseen 'support' of God can make a huge difference.

If we will let him, God can provide us with the loving support we all need so badly. Maybe one of the reasons why there seems to be so much depression around is that people either don't know the love of God or have a relationship with a distorted God of their own making who just makes them feel inadequate and guilty.

There is a moving poem by Mary Stevenson which conveys how God walks beside us, like footprints in the sand. Looking back at the scenes of her life, she saw that there were usually two sets of footprints in the sand, one belonging to her and one to the Lord. But she was puzzled by the fact that at the lowest points in her life there was only one set of footprints. She asked about it and received the reply: 'When you saw only one set of footprints, it was then that I carried you.'

*Question:*
*Think back over when God, or friends, have helped you get through difficult times.*

## Spiritual Aspects

Let us now pull some threads together about spiritual aspects of depression. To find a way out of depression we need all the resources we can muster, including spiritual resources. Depression calls for two of the greatest Christian virtues: love and hope. We have seen the role of hope; it usually comes from a deep place and can have extraordinary staying power in difficult circumstances.

Love is important, too. As we have also seen, we are less at risk of depression if we feel loved and supported, so love is a key factor in the battle against depression. It is when we are close to depression that we most need the love of other people, and of God. Equally, the more we can extend such love to other people, the less they will be at risk of depression.

The kind of love we need in difficult times is very practical. I have long been fond of Charles Andrews' definition of Christian love as 'the accurate estimate and supply of another's need'. It is refreshingly unsentimental, and points us beyond the distortions of love that reflect our own emotional needs. I assume that God sees people's needs accurately, so the kind of love that Andrews is pointing to brings people into alignment with God's perspective. Religious people are committed to love (even though, being human, they sometimes fail to show it). If a community of religious people can really provide the kind of love that reflects the love of God, it will incidentally help to ward off depression.

Once again, let us set aside any idea that depression is a punishment from God, or a sign that a person's faith is not strong enough. Even St Paul, a person of remarkable faith, referred to the affliction he had experienced in Asia when 'we were so utterly, unbearably crushed that we despaired of life itself' (2 Corinthians 1:8).

Even among those who have a sense of a guiding providence in life, it can make a difference whether or not they call it 'God'. We noted earlier how, when people are depressed, they put bad things down to their own failings, and write off good things as mere chance. Having a sense of providence puts that in a broader context. Having a sense of the providence of God seems to soften the very negative view of ourselves that results from blaming ourselves for the bad things, and the inflated self-view that results from taking credit for the good things. A sense of providence softens all that and helps to liberate us from the more unwelcome consequences, such as depression.

Perhaps the greatest value of depression, at least potentially, is that it can force us to face fundamental issues. People can go for years living at a superficial level and not addressing what would really give them a deep sense of satisfaction and fulfilment. If depression leads people to face such issues, it can be a blessing in the long term. Though depression is painful, it can also give us depth of soul. Light can shine more strongly in us when we have wrestled with the darkness of depression and come through it. We come through 'tried as in the fire' (1 Peter 1:7). That doesn't justify depression; it is not something to wish on anyone. However, those who suffer it can come through it with stronger faith and with deeper soul life.

Going into depression has echoes of Jesus going to his crucifixion. He didn't deny how painful it would be, but trusted in God to bring him through it and restore him to life. In doing so he won a battle over darkness and despair. Similarly, we can also come through depression more fully alive, having faced down our demons.

*Question:*
*How could it help you to focus more on the spiritual side of depression?*

## Bible Study

There are periods of what must have been depression in the story of Joseph, when he is thrown into a pit and abandoned by his brothers (Genesis 37:12–36), and when he is imprisoned in Egypt (Genesis 39:1–41:32). See Sara Savage (2011) *Joseph: Insights for the Spiritual Journey*. SPCK. Chapter two.

The Psalms again provide a good expression of what we would now call depression. We referred to Psalm 102, but there are many other Psalms that give depression a voice, such as Psalm 39 or 69.

The suffering servant in Isaiah (52:13–53:12) gives a vivid picture of a suffering comparable to that of someone who is deeply depressed, but there is at least a hint that something good may come of all this suffering, that 'out of his anguish he shall see light' (53:11).

St Paul has quite a lot to say about hope, in the Letter to the Romans, for example. There are two key passages: 5:1–5 and 8:18–25; also the powerful verse 'May the God of hope fill you with all joy and peace in believing, so that you may abound in hope by the power of the Holy Spirit' (Romans 15:13). Reading such verses gives a powerful sense of being sustained by a hope that is bigger than ourselves.

Both St Paul and St John have much to say about the power of love, even if they don't refer explicitly to the power of authentic love to ward off depression. St Paul's great hymn to love (1 Corinthians 13:8–13 is well known). John has a counterpart in 1 John 3:11–24.

## Background and Sources

There has been a huge amount of work recently on the cognitive approach to depression, both on the kind of negative thinking that is such a feature of depression and on the methods of cognitive therapy used to address it. This is set out in many books that are broadly comparable. An example is Paul Gilbert (2009) *Overcoming Depression: A Self-Help Guide Using Cognitive Behavioural Techniques*. Robinson.

The psychological literature on hope is less good, and often labels as 'hopelessness' what I would call pessimism. The best book on the difference between hope and optimism is Terry Eagleton (2015) *Hope Without Optimism*. Yale University Press. Viktor Frankl found ways to maintain hope in a Nazi concentration camp. See his 1946 book, *Man's Search for Meaning*. Rider.

There are also not many books on spiritual aspects of depression, but try Stephanie Sorrell (2009) *Depression as a Spiritual Journey*. O Books. Dorothy Rowe also writes about depression in a way that connects with spirituality. See (1996) *Choosing not Losing: The Experience of Depression*. HarperCollins. Also (1996) *Depression: The Way Out of Your Prison*. 2nd edition. Routledge.

A good resource on depression, which has chapters on almost every aspect, is Ian Gotlib and Constance Hammen (eds.) (2002) *Handbook of Depression*. 3rd edition. Guilford Press.

# Chapter Four
## *Loss and Death*

## Loss

Loss runs through human life and it is one of the hardest things to cope with. At the very beginning of life, most of us feel cared for by our parents, but then they sometimes go away and leave us alone. At first we have no understanding of why that happens, and no ability to do anything about it. Bewilderment and helplessness are intertwined with our experience of loss from the outset.

We have to cope with many losses through life, and they are very varied. People who were important to us move away or lose interest in us; or their circumstances change in some fundamental way, so that they don't seem the same people whom we once depended on. Marriage may give some stability for a time, but partners can change over time, just like anyone else, and eventually they die (unless we die first).

There is also the loss of our hopes. Through life we pin our hopes on various people, groups, causes or beliefs. But, sadly, our hopes are often disappointed, and the loss of hopes can be as cruel as any other loss. It is not only individuals, but whole societies who struggle with the loss of their hopes. It seems an inescapable part of the political process that leaders get hopes up, but then can't fulfil the hopes they have raised.

We also lose aspects of our own lives, or even our very selves. There may be physical loss as we become ill; we may lose a part of our bodies in an accident. For some people whose work has been important to them, retirement is difficult to bear. We can lose our mental faculties as we get old. Ageing involves multiple losses. There are also losses of employment, or of status and position in society, or loss of the respect in which we were once held. And eventually we lose even our lives.

Loss is a central theme in the stories about Jesus and those around him. People come to him for help when faced with their own losses, and he has losses of his own, such as the death of his friend Lazarus (John 11). Eventually he faces the loss of his own life in his crucifixion, and his friends and followers face the loss of him as an everyday companion.

How are we to cope with loss? There are basically two contrasting strategies. One is to try to minimise the experience of loss in our lives. We try to protect ourselves through insurance policies, contracts of employment or other bureaucratic arrangements. Similarly, we can try to protect ourselves against the loss of people who are important to us by institutional arrangements such as marriage, or through various attempts at emotional manipulation. I am generally not very impressed by the effectiveness of trying to manage loss; things come and go, and our efforts to stop that happening often seem like Canute trying to stop the tide coming in.

The other approach starts with an acceptance of the reality of loss. Rather than trying to prevent loss, we try to find better ways of coping with it, ways of staying resilient through loss, and rebuilding what we can on the far side of it. That approach generally seems to sit more easily with a spiritual life. It is also the one that Jesus endorses in one of his core sayings: 'For those who want to save their life will lose it, and those who lose their life for my sake will find it' (Matthew 16:25).

Several of the stories Jesus told seem to advise against the strategy of trying to secure what we have (whether that is money, goods in a barn, or whatever) in the hope of accruing more. Rather, they advise a strategy of risking what we have in the hope of gaining something better.

It is a recommendation that sits well with the psychology of C.G. Jung and his endorsement of sacrificing the rather limited life of our 'ego', the centre of our conscious life, in the hope of making a reality of what he calls the 'Self', the higher and more complete person we have the capacity to become.

*Question:*
*What losses have been hardest to cope with in your life?*

# Bereavement

Though losses are many and varied, the loss of those close to us through death is perhaps the paradigmatic loss, so I turn now to how people cope with bereavement; it is something that comes to everyone. Coping with bereavement also illustrates how people cope with disturbing emotions and difficult experiences in a range of situations.

How hard bereavement is depends on various things, such as how close you were to the person who has died, how old they were, and whether or not their death was expected. The tragic death of children can be particularly tough, but so can the death of a spouse who has been your close, lifelong companion. Sudden death for which we have had no opportunity to prepare is particularly problematic.

People's emotional reactions to bereavement are complex and the balance between different emotions can shift over time. Sometimes these have been seen as 'stages' of grieving, though people seldom move cleanly from one stage to the next. Nevertheless, the so-called stages of grieving show the range of reactions people show, moving through:

*Denial*: At first, people often simply can't believe that the person has died and try to carry on as though they had not. They may feel numbed emotionally. People need time to work through denial and it needs to be handled gently. (Not being able to believe that the person has died is different, of course, from believing in continued existence in some form of afterlife.)

*Anger*: Anger can be expressed at particular people or, more generally, at God, fate, the Church etc. People often ask, 'What have I done to deserve this?', though that is usually not a question to which they want an answer. If bereaved people are angry, be aware that it is often more an expression of their pain. If they are angry at God, it often reveals an idea of God who is controlling every single thing in Creation. That is not what Christians believe, though it is unwise to pick an argument about it with bereaved people.

*Guilt*: People often have big regrets after the death of a loved one and wish they had treated them better. It is a particular feature when the relationship has been ambivalent or conflicted, and can be a major problem in getting over the bereavement. There are usually things to regret, of course, but the guilt is often disproportionate to any actual shortcomings.

*Depression*: As these other reactions subside, the enduring feeling is often just one of sadness at the emptiness of life without the person who has died. This is entirely natural, of course, and working through it is often a slow business. However, there is a difference between understandable sadness and more extreme despair that tips over into depression.

There is often an intense relationship with the person who has just died, but one in which emotions predominate. The deceased person still seems very much present, and the bereaved person goes on relating to them as though they were still actually there. Later, there is more detachment and objectivity; it becomes possible to remember the deceased person more clearly, and to think *about* them in a more accurate way than is possible in the early stages of bereavement. All this has been beautifully described by C.S. Lewis in his account of the grief he experienced after the death of his wife.

There is an interesting parallel between everyday bereavement reactions, such as those of Lewis, and the remarks attributed to Jesus in John's Gospel (the so-called Farewell Discourses, John 14–16), in which Jesus prepares his disciples for life without him as an everyday companion. The sense of understanding more clearly the significance of Jesus' words after he has gone is not atypical of bereavement, as is the increasing veneration of Jesus after his death. The Spirit of Jesus will help them through and there is also a conviction that they will see Jesus again, and that all will end well.

*Question:*
*What do you find most painful about bereavement?*

## Know Your Feelings

There are many situations in life that arouse strong feelings. Bereavement is one example; it gives rise to anger, guilt, depression and more. However, there are many other things that produce strong emotions. How should we handle our emotions for the best?

People have very different approaches to their feelings. Some people are more aware of them than others; some people express them more than others. Quite a range of different approaches to emotions can work. Problems arise mainly at the two extremes, but of different kinds.

There are some advantages in being very controlled about your feelings. In some ways you may be able to cope with stress better if you can 'keep a stiff upper lip'. But there is a price to be paid. If you are too controlled you may not engage fully with what is going on around you. Some situations can be handled in a detached way, but there are other situations where you really have to be emotionally engaged, or else you completely miss the point. Some people are so controlled about their feelings that they are not even *aware* of their own feelings. Then there is a tendency for feelings to leak out in other ways, for example in physical problems.

Different problems arise at the other end of the spectrum where feelings are uncontrolled. Then our feelings just take over in a way that may be dangerous for other people, and even for ourselves. When we are in the grip of emotions, we can easily do things that we regret later. Over the centuries, Christians have been very aware of the problems caused by unbridled passions. Uncontrolled anger or uncontrolled lust can indeed do a lot of damage, and Christians have been right to be aware of that. But excessive guilt or fear can also do a lot of damage, and Christians have been less vigilant about that. Psychology has done more to draw attention to how debilitating excessive guilt or fear can be.

Until recently, there has not been much recognition of how helpful emotions can be (though some Christian thinkers talk about the helpful role of the 'affections', and distinguish them from the 'passions'). Recently there has been much more emphasis on just how much we depend upon our feelings. They are sometimes wiser than our thinking; they often function as a warning sign when something is seriously wrong. They can be useful in energising us in an emergency, and can also help us to change direction quickly in an emergency when we really need to. More important than anything else, our feelings are such an important part of us that, if we try to operate without them, we are only a shadow of our complete selves.

At funerals you see both extremes in how people engage with their feelings. Some people are so controlled that they don't engage with their feelings at all. Others abandon themselves to their feelings so completely that they don't allow the funeral to help them to work things through. Funerals are most helpful to those who are emotionally engaged, but who benefit from the structure and support that a funeral can provide; it helps if they are conducted in a way that enables people to strike that balance. The same applies to all situations where raw emotions are involved.

Humans are emotional creatures, and we are at our best when we are emotionally engaged. But humans also characteristically want to make sense of things, to understand why they feel as they do, and to find appropriate words for their feelings. That involves a to and fro between experiencing our feelings and making sense of things. If we learn how to do that for ourselves, we can help other people do it too, both to help them to be emotionally engaged and to help them to make sense of things.

Feelings are also an important part of religious life. Love of God and compassion for others are cornerstones around which religion is built. Even negative feelings can be useful. Though it can be debilitating to be wracked with excessive guilt, guilt also has a useful role to play and can help us to see that our behaviour reflects our good intentions. There is more to religious life than emotion, but if we are too emotionally detached, our religious life seems to lack proper roots and lack authenticity. Our emotions can serve us well and we are only half ourselves without them, but they become a problem if they take us over completely. They are a good servant but a poor master.

*Question:*

*How in touch are you with your feelings?*

## Loss and Growth

In supporting people through grief it is often hard to know what to say. Sadly, that sometimes leads people to shun those who are bereaved. It is also unhelpful to give too much advice, and best to just show kindness and concern, to give practical help if that is wanted, and to provide a listening ear.

As people come through the grief, they become more ready to find the new opportunities that the loss opens up. That may involve finding new friends and new activities, and developing a new identity. Someone who has experienced loss has to find their own way through it, but in doing so they will benefit from support and encouragement.

There are two sides to all losses: one is coming to terms with what has been lost, the other is building up something new. Loss is initially negative, but it can end up being positive. There can be gains as well as losses. There can be both loss and growth. It is important to keep the balance between the two, not denying the loss, but also recognising that good can come out of loss.

There has been growing recognition in recent years of what is known as 'post-traumatic growth'. Traumatic experiences of many different kinds can lead to significant shifts in people's attitudes, thinking and use of time. Such changes can be very significant and can lead to new priorities, warmer and more intimate relationships, a new sense of opportunities for spiritual development, and a greater sense of personal strength and appreciation of life.

Some form of post-traumatic growth is common; indeed the vast majority of people who have been through a trauma or loss or some kind say that they have experienced some kind of growth as a result of it. Such growth seems to be strongest in people who are open to experience and who are able to accept what has happened to them, rather than just feeling aggrieved about it. It helps to be hopeful about the future. As I said in the last chapter, hope is more important than optimism.

It helps to have someone close to you to talk things over with, and to help you to find points of growth. That often involves making sense of things and developing a story about how the trauma has helped you. Making sense of things seems to be crucial to coming through a difficult experience with a sense of being enhanced in some way.

Post-traumatic growth is closely linked with spirituality. Spiritual people are more likely to show post-traumatic growth, and post-traumatic growth usually takes people in a more spiritual direction. The concept of post-traumatic growth is closely parallel to beliefs found in many religious traditions. For Christians, it will be seen as similar to the core belief that 'crucifixion' (which can take many forms) can be followed by resurrection.

Baptism is another powerful symbol of loss and growth; the symbolism is clearest when there is immersion in the water, perhaps in a river. Going down under the water is a symbol of loss or surrender of a previous way of living. Coming up out of the water again is a symbol of the gain or growth that comes with making a fresh start. It is a kind of resurrection, or post-traumatic growth.

In many societies, rituals to do with loss and change have been found to involve a door or gateway. Experiencing loss seems to be like going through a doorway, leaving one room behind and coming out into another. When Jesus was talking about a sheepfold, he said that he himself was the gate: 'I am the gate for the sheep . . . whoever enters by me will be saved, and will come in and go out and find pasture' (John 10:7–9). For many people, Jesus is the gate that leads from trauma or loss to a better future, with more spiritual depth.

> *Question:*
> *Think what good has come of losses you have experienced.*

## Dying

The biggest loss any of us will face is death, the loss of our own lives. It is the ultimate loss. In the first half of life it is something most people hardly think about but, from mid-life onwards, there is an increasing element of preparation for death in many people's lives.

One strand in that is a kind of stocktaking. Long before we get to death, it can be helpful to stop and think how you would like to be remembered after your death, and to compare that with how you would probably be remembered if you died now. For most of us, there is quite a big gap between the two. Reflecting on that can help us to lead our lives better and to set clearer priorities for ourselves.

Some people fear death. Part of that is fear of the actual process of dying, which is quite often painful. There can also be fear of what will come after death. The instinct to fear death is very deep-seated but, from a religious perspective, long life is not the most important objective. The quality of life, and what use we make of whatever life is given us, is more important than how long we live. For Christians, the sense of being united with Christ is more important than long life, and that is not affected by death. As St Paul put it, 'If we live, we live to the Lord, and if we die, we die to the Lord; so then, whether we live or whether we die, we are the Lord's' (Romans 14:8).

Funerals continue to play an important role in society and, at least for now, the number of funerals has declined less steeply than the number of weddings and baptisms. There is still a strong instinct that a church funeral is the right way to pay respect to the departed. But that creates a situation in which most of those who attend funerals are not sure what to think about the afterlife.

Even if people have some instinctive sympathy with the idea of an afterlife, they are not sure how to express that, or why they believe in it. That often gives a strange disconnect between the theology of death in the public funeral rite and the private thoughts of those present. I have rarely attended a funeral service where the whole community is confident of their belief in the afterlife but, when I have, it feels completely different.

For many people, how Jesus approached his own death is a helpful example. He was courageous and matter-of-fact in facing death. He was willing to sacrifice his life, believing that was what he was called to do. He went to Jerusalem knowing that he would die there, when he could have stayed safely in Galilee. He didn't try to hide from the guards on the night of his arrest. He was obviously not running scared of death, but facing it bravely.

On the other hand, Jesus did not seek death eagerly, as some martyrs have done. He seems to have been under no illusions about how painful it would be. Shortly before his arrest, he prayed that, if possible, he would be spared it, spared having to drink this 'cup' (Luke 22:42). Jesus neither sought death nor avoided it, but seems to have approached it in a matter-of-fact spirit, as something he had to go through.

When Christians face difficult circumstances, they can connect with Jesus who has also been there. However much pain we are having to bear as we approach death, it is unlikely to be worse than the pain of crucifixion. However much we feel betrayed, it is unlikely to be worse than Jesus' betrayal by Judas and the many others who had cheered him only a few days previously. The hymn 'My Song is Love Unknown' puts it well: 'Sometimes they strew his way and his sweet praises sing, resounding all the day Hosannas to their King. Then "Crucify!" is all their breath, and for his death they thirst and cry.'

There is a sense in which Jesus is present, across the gulf of time and space, whenever there is a painful and unjust death. Elie Wiesel told the story of watching a child hanging on the gallows in a concentration camp, and dying very slowly. He heard someone ask, 'For God's sake, where is God?', and heard a voice within him answer, 'Where He is? This is where – hanging here from this gallows.'

There can also be a connection between Jesus' path to death and our own. It would help many people to steer the middle path to death that Jesus took, neither seeking death eagerly and enthusiastically out of religious conviction, nor running scared of it and trying to hide from it; but just facing it, however difficult and painful, calmly and confidently.

> *Question:*
> *Are you frightened of dying? If so, how do you cope with that?*

## Bible Study

The story of Joseph is again a good basis for reflection on loss. Think about Joseph's loss of connection with his family and how he regained it (Genesis 43:15–45:24); and for his approach to death see Genesis 45:16–50:26. See again Sara Savage (2011) *Joseph: Insights for the Spiritual Journey*. SPCK. Chapters five and six.

Read all or part of what Jesus says to his disciples to prepare them for life beyond his crucifixion (John 14–16, or perhaps just John 16:16–24), and how Jesus says that their sorrow will turn to joy.

Read the story of Mary Magdalene feeling bereaved after Jesus' crucifixion (20:1–18), and follow her through her journey to a sense of life and joy.

Read what Jesus says about being the door to the sheepfold (John 10:9–18) and ponder whether and how he can be the door between our life before loss and trauma and our life afterwards.

Read what St Paul says about baptism being a transition from death to life (Romans 6:3–10) and ponder whether life beyond trauma and growth can be like coming up out of the waters of baptism.

## Background and Sources

On emotionality, see Daniel Goleman (1996) *Emotional Intelligence*. Bloomsbury Publishing. This is the classic book introducing the concept of 'emotional intelligence'; there are many books following up on the idea, with guidelines for how to improve yours. The concept of emotional intelligence has caught on in the popular imagination, despite some scepticism among scientists about whether it really is 'intelligence', whether it really helps people to succeed as claimed etc. See also Robert Augustus Masters (2013) *Emotional Intimacy: A Comprehensive Guide for Connecting with the Power of Your Emotions*. Sounds True. (A useful practical guide to connecting better with your emotions.)

On post-traumatic growth, see M. Craig Barnes (1996) *When God Interrupts: Finding New Life through Unwanted Change.* Inter-Varsity Press. Also Michaela Haas (2015). *Bouncing Forward: Transforming Bad Breaks into Breakthroughs.* Atria/Enliven. (An accessible account of post-traumatic growth, connecting it with Buddhist spirituality.)

There is helpful background material on death and dying in Fraser Watts, Rebecca Nye and Sara Savage (2002) *Psychology for Christian Ministry.* Routledge. Chapter eight. Other useful books on death and bereavement are:

C.S. Lewis (1961) *A Grief Observed.* Faber and Faber. (A very carefully observed personal account of bereavement.)

Colin Murray Parkes (2010) *Bereavement: Studies of Grief in Adult Life.* 4th edition. Penguin. (A classic psychological account of bereavement.)

Robert Kastenbaum (2000) *The Psychology of Death.* 3rd edition. Free Association Books. A classic wide-ranging survey of psychological research relevant to death.

Nicholas Peter Harvey (1985) *Death's Gift: Chapters on Resurrection and Bereavement.* Epworth Press. (Connects Jesus' Farewell Discourses with the process of bereavement.)

Douglas Davies (1997/2017) *Death, Ritual and Belief.* Bloomsbury Academic. (An important sociological and theological study of death and dying.)

# Chapter Five
## *Suffering, Illness and Wholeness*

## Why Suffering?

We all have difficult times in our lives, times of loss, failure, disappointment or rejection, times when we feel wounded and suffer. There is no way of avoiding such times; they are part of the stuff of life. Some people experience more suffering than others, but no one avoids it entirely.

When people suffer they often instinctively want to ask: 'Why?' 'What have I done to deserve this?' Why me?' Behind these questions is often the idea that God has decided that we should suffer. Then they feel indignant, because it seems unreasonable or unfair. Let us first examine that question. Actually, it may not really be a question at all; people probably don't really want an answer to it. Asking the question is probably more a way of making a protest than asking a real question. But the question arises from some tangled and mistaken assumptions that are worth examining.

Some people imagine that because they are Christians they will be exempt from suffering, or that if they suffer it means their faith isn't strong enough. This is a complete misunderstanding. God does not promise freedom from suffering, so we should never judge ourselves, or others, because we suffer. Suffering can't be taken as a sign of weak faith or of God's displeasure.

There is also sometimes another misunderstanding that God has decided that we should suffer. Christians believe that all Creation owes its existence to God, and that God loves it, guides it and nurtures it. However, they also believe that God has granted freedom to Creation, and that God is not controlling it or micro-managing it. So, if we suffer, it is not because God has decided that we should.

What God does promise is to stay with us through suffering and help to see us through. Christians find an example of this in Jesus. He certainly suffers, especially in his trial and crucifixion, but he triumphs over his suffering in a way that has been an inspiration to countless people ever since. He is a model of how we can grow through suffering, of how it can bring benefits.

It is instructive to watch how Jesus approaches suffering. He anticipates the appalling suffering of crucifixion more clearly than most people are able to do, but he approaches it in a calm, purposeful matter-of-fact way. There are two extremes that he avoids. One is shrinking from the suffering that is facing him, or running away from it. The other is going to his suffering cheerfully, in a way that denies the appalling reality of suffering. There is already an achievement in how Jesus approaches the suffering involved in his crucifixion.

If people approach suffering in the right way, they can be enriched by it. It may seem strange to suggest that people can benefit from suffering or trauma, but quite often they do. Not always, of course; sometimes people can be so crushed by suffering that they never quite recover. But for many people, suffering brings change and growth.

As we have already seen, psychologists have gathered evidence for what they call 'post-traumatic growth'. There is now much evidence of people growing through war, natural disaster and personal setbacks. It is not an automatic response to suffering or trauma, but depends on how people square up to the challenge of rebuilding their lives after a time of suffering.

People can emerge from a traumatic period with new priorities, greater confidence, better relationships and a sense of new possibilities. Often there is spiritual change too. Whether or not people turn to conventional religion, they often emerge from trauma or suffering with a stronger focus on ultimate or transcendent values and priorities.

*Question:*
*Can any good come from human suffering?*
*Can you think of any examples?*

## Health and Illness

Suffering sometimes takes the form of illness. We have already looked at stress, anxiety, depression and loss. We will now look at physical illness.

Once again, illness should not be seen as a punishment from God. In a story in the Gospels, Jesus refuses to blame either a blind man or his parents for being blind (John 6). It is not in God's nature to decide that particular people should get ill. He doesn't have that kind of relationship with Creation. God has given Creation its freedom. Religious people can get ill, just like anyone else.

Nevertheless, there is a trend for religious people to have better health than others, and to come through it better if they do get ill. It is only one factor, but the evidence for it is now quite strong. Why should religion be good for physical health? There are various possible explanations.

One is that religious people tend to have healthier lifestyles, for example to be less likely to eat and drink excessively, less likely to smoke, less likely to be overweight etc. Religion tends to be associated with a healthy lifestyle, and that makes them less likely to get ill. Religion may well also be associated with being responsive to health advice and complying with treatment regimes.

Religious people are also likely to be part of good, supportive networks of people who care about each other and look after each other. Of course, many non-religious people have good networks too, and not all religious communities are as supportive as they might be. Still, there is a trend for religious people to have better social support, and that can also contribute to better physical health.

Certain religious practices can also be good for health. Prayer and meditation tend to be good for people in various ways. For one thing they provide a daily period of quiet and calm that is likely to be good for health. Prayer also provides an opportunity to reflect on events in one's life and make sense of them. We all experience things that are puzzling and difficult, and raw events that we can make no sense of are bad for our health and can cause suffering. At the heart of the religious life is the regular effort to make sense of what is happening to us in relation to the purposes of God. That process of finding meaning in things is likely to be good for our health.

A wide range of virtues are associated with good health too, including forgiveness, gratitude, altruism, hope and so on. Such virtues are partly a matter of inner emotional state, and partly a style of social interaction. Both could contribute to health in different ways.

Religion can also help with pain. The experience of pain depends on two rather different factors. It partly depends, of course, on the amount of tissue damage in the area concerned. However, it also depends on psychological processes that are connected with the central nervous system.

We saw that depression is made worse by getting upset about being depressed. In a similar way, pain is made worse by being upset about pain. An attitude of acceptance is likely not only to help us to bear pain, it also actually reduces the level of pain we experience. Being good at making sense of things will also probably help with pain, and religion helps with that.

Religion helps in different ways with different health problems. There are some specific effects on top of the general factors we have been looking at so far. We can illustrate this with two of the most common illnesses in modern society – cancer and heart problems.

The most important risk factors for cardiac problems are to do with aspects of lifestyle: eating, drinking, smoking, exercise etc. In as far as religion reduces the risk of cardiac problems, it is likely to be largely through such factors. Another risk factor is high blood pressure and a rather driven (type A) personality. Emotional factors are likely to be more relevant with that. If religious practices like meditation induce a certain calmness, they are likely to reduce cardiac risk by another route.

Emotional factors seem to be important with cancer too, but the pathway by which that works is not so obvious. The connections are quite complex and we are only just beginning to see how it works, but it looks as though the basic story is something like this. Cancer is a matter of cells in the body over-reproducing themselves. There are internal processes that normally stop that happening, but which sometimes break down. Those regulative processes are mediated through our immune system. That in turn seems to be associated with our emotional state, and problems in regulating anger are linked to how the immune system functions.

So, if religion affects our emotional state, that in turn affects our immune system, which can affect how cancerous cells reproduce. Needless to say, there is much more research to be done to check out that possible route by which religion could affect cancer.

> *Question:*
>
> *How can religion be good for your health?*
> *How could it help with your own health problems?*

## Healing

When people get ill, there can be special prayers for healing. Sometimes laying on of hands, or anointing, are used along with prayer. Such spiritual healing can now be found both in many religious circles and it can also be found with healers in the 'new age' movement who use similar techniques, but outside a framework of conventional belief.

The effects of such spiritual healing are difficult to assess scientifically, but it does often seem to have helpful effects. It is not as simple and predictable as taking medication, although too many people have experienced some kind of spiritual healing for it to be easily dismissed. There really do seem to be benefits.

However, what is going on in spiritual healing, and why people benefit from it, is more complex. Some people will say that it obviously proves the power of God. Others may say that benefits are entirely psychological and that there is nothing specifically religious about it at all. My own view is that there is a complex mixture of things going on that are not easy to sort out.

Let us start with some of the more obvious and uncontroversial things. People who engage in spiritual healing usually believe in what they are doing. The fact that they believe in it helps it to work. If you have faith that you will be healed, it is more likely that you will be healed. The effects of all attempts to heal people seem to be enhanced if people believe in them. That applies to spiritual healing, too. In that obvious sense, it is 'faith' healing.

The focus of that faith may vary. It can be primarily in God, or in the healer, or in the process of healing and what the healer does.

People probably don't normally make too sharp a distinction between them; there is an element of faith in God, in the healer and in the healing process.

Sometimes people seem to 'go through the motions' of praying for healing, without much passion or urgency, and without much expectation that it will make any difference. I doubt whether that kind of spiritual healing does much good. Jesus is quite clear that people who pray should pray with passion and urgency, and tells stories to make that point, like the story of the person who needs bread in the middle of the night and bangs on his neighbour's door so long and hard that the poor man gets up and gives him what he needs (Luke 11:5–10). If we want healing prayer to work, we should take it seriously and put time and effort into it.

There are probably also some biological aspects to spiritual healing. If healing affects the body, there are bound to be physiological processes that mediate its effects. Some aspects of the healing process may specifically contribute to the biological processes through which the effects of healing are mediated. There is often physical contact in spiritual healing which may contribute to its effects. Our primate ancestors spend much time in mutual grooming which probably had a variety of helpful effects, some of which may contribute to spiritual healing. Religious dancing or other rituals may induce an unusual state of consciousness, in which people are less controlled than usual, and more open to experience. That may also contribute to healing.

There is now good reason to think that spiritual practices such as prayer and meditation are good for health, and so may contribute to the benefits of spiritual healing. They have effects on both mind and body that can be beneficial.

I mention all these different ways in which spiritual healing could be beneficial to make the point that it is not at all surprising that spiritual healing is often helpful. You don't have to believe in God to recognise that there are many ways in which spiritual healing can be helpful. There is nothing incredible about it, even for those who don't believe in God.

However, I don't want to imply that there is nothing more to spiritual healing than the factors I have mentioned. It seems likely that there is some energy for healing that flows from God. When two or more people pray together for healing with passion and urgency they connect with that energy, and it flows with new power and impact.

Personally, I have two different ways of approaching spiritual healing. I can stand back and look with cool detachment at how it might work, as I have in this section. However, when someone asks me to pray for healing for them, I instinctively set that aside and focus solely on invoking the healing power of Christ with all the passion and conviction I can muster. When I do that, the results are often impressive.

> *Question:*
>
> *Can prayer restore people to health?*
> *Do you sometimes seek prayer when you are ill?*

## Wholeness

Our instinctive response to suffering is to want to get rid of it. That is natural, and there is certainly nothing good about suffering in itself. But there is another deeper response to suffering than just wanting to get rid of it, which is, 'How can this suffering become a source of blessing to me?'

Entering a time of suffering is like going through a door, or into a tunnel. It may at first be dark and forbidding, but it can sometimes lead us into a brighter place. On the far side of the tunnel of suffering, there can be a bright and beautiful garden. It is like going from a prison into freedom. So, if we find ourselves suffering, let us ask how we can turn it to our advantage and grow through it. If we do that, we will be following in the path of Jesus, who turned the suffering of the cross to the new life of Resurrection.

There is more to healing than just getting rid of suffering. Healing literally means making us 'whole', and there is more to becoming whole people than just getting rid of suffering. It may involve learning to bear our suffering in a way that is fruitful for ourselves and others. If we learn to bear one suffering fruitfully, it will help us to bear other sufferings if need be; in that sense it is a 'transferable skill'.

Our relationship with God can help us learn how suffering can become a source of blessing. For that, we need to work in collaboration with God, not imagining that we can do it all ourselves, nor leaving it entirely to him, but working in partnership with God. Sometimes our suffering arises from things we were doing ourselves that were self-destructive and caused us suffering. Then, the wisest course of action may simply be to take ourselves in hand and correct what is causing us to suffer.

But sometimes there are dark sides of our personality that can be healed, redirected and put to good use, rather than simply eliminated. There have always been two rather different strands of religious teaching jostling together on this. One wants to identify the parts of us that are leading us astray and to get rid of them, so that what remains is pure and righteous. The other wants to heal and redeem even most the problematic parts of us. There is probably a time for both, but my sympathies are more with the latter approach. Let me explain why.

Partly it is just a practical judgement. I am doubtful whether we can actually get rid of the problematic parts of ourselves. Even if we control one manifestation of them, we can find that they have gone underground, changed their spots, and are now causing trouble in other ways. So, as a psychologist, I am doubtful about this strategy.

I also have doubts from a religious point of view about whether it is an appropriate thing even to attempt. Looked at in that way, I don't think there is anything in Creation that can't be healed and redeemed, so that it can contribute to the purposes of God. As the old marriage service said, we can hope that our 'natural instincts and affections, implanted by God, should be hallowed and directed aright'. Even what may seem to be our darkest side can be put to good use within the broader framework of God's purposes.

Making sense of things that are causing us suffering, through putting them in the bigger picture of God's purposes, can be very important in bringing healing and wholeness. For suffering to lead to wholeness we need to come to understand how it can find a place in the bigger picture of our lives.

*Question:*
*What would the signs of 'wholeness' be for you?*

## Social Wholeness

So far we have been looking at this question of suffering and wholeness from the point of view of the individual, but we will now broaden out to look at the road from suffering to wholeness in families, communities and whole societies. We will look more fully at issues of relationship and society in the next section but, for now, let us see how the theme of wholeness applies to society as well as the individual.

Much suffering comes from a breakdown in human relationships, and it is very important to find a way from suffering to a restoration of wholeness in communities too, at all levels.

There are various ways in which relations break down. We can become insensitive to the consequences of our actions for other people, and become so locked in our egocentricity, our own point of view and our own desires, that we cause damage to other people.

Disagreements can become so polarised that we no longer look for consensus but exaggerate our disagreements. A disagreement over one thing can become over-generalised, so we start to imagine that we disagree over everything. We start to divide people up into those that are like us and those that are unlike us. Then we scapegoat those who are not like us, attributing everything bad to them, and make them out to be the source of all our problems.

Wholeness of society is very hard to achieve. There seems to be a natural instinct, when we are anxious and feeling under threat, to bunker down, look for security and solidarity with people like ourselves, and to see people unlike ourselves as the source of all our problems. What happened in Nazi Germany is a warning of how that process can get out of hand; and there are similar forces at work now that are quite dangerous.

The solution to this lies partly in recognising and rejoicing in diversity, rather than allowing it to become a source of disagreement and division. When we are not feeling beleaguered, we can celebrate diversity in a way that overcomes division and the suffering it brings, and restores wholeness to relationships and communities.

Jesus tells a story about a fold of sheep from which one has gone missing. The shepherd makes it a priority to find the lost sheep and bring it back into the fold, so that the fold will be full and complete. It is basically a story about wholeness, about going to great lengths to gather everything together into a unity. It encourages us to go and look for the lost parts of our personalities and bring them back into the fold, and to look for the lost members of our community or the ones that we have been scapegoating and to bring them back too.

After telling the story, Jesus says that he has other sheep that are not of this fold, and he wants to gather them in too. Some of those sheep may seem so 'other' to us that they are hardly acceptable in the fold. But yet Jesus wants to gather them all in, in his search for wholeness. In the end, such wholeness, both of personality and society, is in the best interest of all of us. Jesus' work is to gather everything in.

> *Question:*
> *How can we go about building wholeness in society?*

## Bible Study

One of the most vivid accounts of suffering in the Bible is St Paul's description of his own sufferings in 2 Corinthians 11:23–31. Jesus also talked to his disciples, in Mark 10:32–34, about all that he was going to suffer. How would you have felt if you had suffered such things? How did Jesus and St Paul feel, and can you learn from them about how to bear your own sufferings?

There are also some moving visions of wholeness in the Bible, such as the vision of peace and harmony in Isaiah 65:17–25, or the vision of paradise in Revelation 22:1–7. It was Jesus' explicit purpose to establish this comprehensive wholeness (Luke 7:22). The healing of the flesh of individuals is a sign of the more general wholeness that God desires and promises. The healing of Naaman in the Jordan is one of the most vivid healing stories in the Bible (2 Kings 5:1–15).

## Background and Sources

There are many books exploring the problems of evil and suffering. They mostly cover similar ground, but one that is particularly clear-headed is Brian Hebblethwaite (2000) *Evil, Suffering and Religion*. SPCK. See also Philip Yancey (2001) *Where is God When it Hurts?* Zondervan. For a more psychological approach see John A. Sanford (1982) *Evil: The Shadow Side of Reality*. Independent Publishers Group.

I have reviewed research on religion and health in chapter eleven of Fraser Watts (2017) *Psychology, Religion and Spirituality*. Cambridge University Press. I have also brought together various perspectives on healing in Fraser Watts (ed.) (2011) *Spiritual Healing: Scientific and Religious Perspectives*. Cambridge University Press. I will have more to say about healing of the body in a book on Embodied Spirituality, to be published shortly by SCM Press.

A classic that integrates the various different spiritual streams that converge in healing is John A. Sanford (1977) *Healing and Wholeness*. Paulist Press. On wholeness see Anna F. Lemkow (1990) *The Wholeness Principle: Dynamics of Unity Within Science, Religion and Society*. Quest Books.

# Section Two
## *Relationships and Community*

# Chapter Six
## *Personal Relationships*

## The Place of Relationships

Relationships are important for human beings. We are all shaped by relationships and need relationships. Equally, our relationships with other people are important for them.

People differ in how they relate to others. There are different but equally valid ways of going about relationships. For example, some of us are introverts and prefer few but special friends; others are extroverts who connect easily with a wide circle of people. Many of us are some mixture of the two. There is no 'right' or 'wrong' about that. Not everyone needs to be equally sociable; there are quiet and subdued ways of having deep and significant relationships.

There is a healthy to and fro about relationships, an intuitive sense that if someone takes care of us we ought to take care of them. We see something similar in other animals, for example in the way they exchange grooming. One animal grooms another and, when it is done, they switch roles, and the one who has been groomed now does the grooming. That instinct for the exchange of favours seems deeply ingrained.

There is an issue about whether we should exchange like for like in relationships, or whether it works for people to exchange very different things. In recent decades we seem to have been moving towards a social consensus that it is best to exchange like for like, but that has not always been the case. In classical marriages of fifty years ago or more, the normal pattern was of exchanging rather different things: the man's job was material provision and the woman was more concerned with relationships. There is absolutely nothing wrong with such patterns of exchange, but they can lead to resentment.

Many people have mixed feelings about the people they are close to. In some ways, other people can be a great blessing to us; we become very fond of each other and come to depend on one another. However, human nature being what it is, we are often disappointed by the people we are closest to, and we are bound to be a disappointment to them. For many people, relationships are both a blessing and a curse. They raise constant challenges.

Bad relationships can be very damaging. One really bad relationship can cast a long shadow, distorting many other relationships that come after it. It distorts how we see all other relationships. For example, once one person has been abusive towards us, we can easily assume everyone else is going to be abusive too. But, on the other hand, good relationships can be very healing, and a good relationship is often the best way of healing the damage done by a bad relationship.

A small number of religious people seem to opt out of human relationships entirely and become hermits, so that they can focus on their relationship with God. However, even hermits are often not quite as isolated as they seem. They have still been shaped by relationships and carry within them the people with whom they have been most closely connected. Some hermits depend on the support of a monastic community for their life as hermits to be viable.

Christians have a special understanding of the importance of relationships within the Godhead; they see the importance of relationships in human life as reflecting the place of relationships within God. For Christians, God is comprised of three distinct persons (Father, Son and Spirit), who are in relationship with one another, engaged in a 'dance of love' with one another. Christians see humans as being called to a similar dance of love with God and with one another.

Human relationships are not quite the same as the relationships between Father, Son and Spirit. We humans have a stronger sense of our separateness and are more divided from one another than the persons of the Trinity are. Nevertheless, our relationality can be at least a pale reflection of the relationality within God; and God provides a model of harmonious relationality for humans to aspire to.

*Question:*
*How much do you depend on other people?*
*How much do they depend on you?*

## Helping Each Other to Flourish

It is important to understand what we need from each other, if life is to go well for us all. Then we can help each person to flourish. Other people can do that for us and we can do it for them. Understanding each other's needs, and trying to meet them, is the essence of practical love. I have already quoted Charles Andrews' definition of love as 'the accurate estimate and supply of another's need'.

Parents need to consider what their children need if they are to grow up well. A lot has been written about how to be good parents, but much of it comes down to combining two things. On the one hand children need to know that their parents love them, care for them and will look after them. On the other hand they need help from their parents in learning that they can't always have their own way, learning to develop self-control, and learning the consequences of their actions.

Children don't grow up well without *both* of these things. Without love and nurture they grow up timid and insecure. People need someone to care for them as plants need the warmth and light of the sun. However, if they receive only love and nurture, but get no help in learning boundaries or self-discipline, they become 'spoiled' children and are often unhappy.

People's relationship with God is most helpful when it combines those two features. Christians believe that God loves us and cares for us more consistently than any human being could. A strong sense of God's love can be very helpful to us. However, God doesn't always indulge us; God can be tough and demanding. We may not like that; but, given the wisdom of God, we stand to benefit from it.

Those involved in counselling have also given careful thought to what people need if they are to change and grow. One helpful approach is that of Carl Rogers, who developed person-centred counselling. He believed that there are three basic conditions people need in counselling if they are to flourish.

Firstly, the counsellor needs to show empathy and the empathy needs to be accurate; people need to feel they are understood. The need to be understood (and feel understood) is one of the most basic of human needs. Without it we easily close down and become unable to function at our best. Of course, understanding people is not straightforward, and it is very easy to make mistakes. If we get it wrong we can easily sound judgemental. So, it is best to tread cautiously, not getting too far ahead of what a person is saying about themselves, until we are sure of our ground.

Secondly, the client needs to feel human warmth, and that the counsellor has a positive attitude to them that is unconditional; they need to feel valued and accepted. Sometimes being 'accurate' about another person involves saying things that are hard to hear. But such things should be very specific. It is essential that they are said kindly, and with real warmth, to ensure that the person does not feel that they are being criticised for what they *are*, but only for some very specific thing they may have said or done. Of course, we don't like everyone equally; we can take more risks with people we really like, and who know that we really like them.

Thirdly, the client needs to sense that the counsellor is being genuine and honest, not just saying the right thing. There have been quite big shifts over the decades in what virtues are most highly valued, and genuineness has been shooting up the league table of highly valued virtues. It sometimes seems now that 'integrity' trumps everything else, and that anything is acceptable provided it is done with integrity. I don't want to go that far, but everyone involved in caring relationships needs to be aware of just how important genuineness now is. It is not enough just to say the right things; we need to be coming from the right place, and people can usually sense whether or not we are.

These three conditions have been shown to help people understand themselves better, and to flourish better as a result of counselling. They provide a model of a good relationship of any kind (though in naturally occurring relationships, people do this for each other; it is not just one way). For Christians, these three conditions sum up the kind of love they feel they receive from God, and which they aim to show to others.

*Question:*
*Think of someone who has shown you understanding, warmth and genuineness.*
*How easily can you show those qualities to others?*

# Attachment and Trust

As children grow up, they need an adult to whom they can become 'attached'; it is usually a parent but it doesn't have to be. What kind of attachment we have to our parents influences us for the rest of our lives. It shapes all the close relationships we form as adults, and our relationship with God.

If things go well, we form a secure attachment in childhood. The figures to whom we become attached are generally seen as strong and wise. We develop close bonds of affection with them and like to stay physically close to them. They provide a safe haven during times of distress and a secure base to which we can return after going off on our own to explore. Ideally they are caring and able to provide for our needs.

However, sometimes there is no suitable adult to whom children can form a secure attachment. That seems to be the case for about a third of the population. A key factor is whether or not potential attachment figures are sensitive to the signals children give about their needs. If parents are unresponsive, attachments become insecure. That shows itself in various ways. Children might avoid the person to whom they are attached, or develop a mixed pattern in which they sometimes approach them and sometimes avoid, or become resistant to the influence of their parents.

The relationship that adults have with God can be seen, in many ways, as like the attachment relationship that infants have with their parents or carers. Just like a good parent, God is seen as stronger and wiser, and someone with whom we can develop close bonds of affection. He is a safe haven to whom we can return in times of difficulty. People often want to stay close to God, but that works a bit differently from how it does with human parents, because God is an unseen presence, and one that can be felt everywhere.

The kind of attachments that people form in infancy persist into adulthood, and influence all our relationships, including our relationship with God. If people have had a strong, secure attachment to their parents, they tend to have that kind of relationship with God. Equally, if children have had an insecure attachment to their parents, it can distort how they relate to God. Sometimes it makes their relationship with God edgy and distrustful. However, if they *can* develop a secure attachment to God, it can compensate for the insecure attachment they had with their parents.

If we have failed to find good, secure attachment relationships as children, we often go on seeking them in adulthood, perhaps especially in the early years of adulthood when there are many changes and transitions to accomplish. Religious leaders are often used as attachment figures, and can offer themselves as such. The Catholic practice of addressing priests as 'Father' makes that explicit, but it probably happens just as much in other denominations, if not so obviously. The tendency for priests to be used as attachment figures places a heavy responsibility on them, and must be used carefully and wisely.

Sometimes people become attached to places in a way that parallels some aspects of attachments to key people. Places (often homes) come to feel like a secure base and a safe haven to which we can return in times of difficulty. Separation from places to which we have become attached can cause distress and lead to a longing to return. Whole societies can become attached to particular places that represent their secure base. Often these place attachments are religious. Mecca is important for Muslims, and Jerusalem for Jews. Much of the Old Testament is the story of how Jews were exiled from Jerusalem when they were taken off into Babylon, and of their longing to return to their beloved Jerusalem.

Attachment is closely intertwined with trust. It helps us to become attached to someone if we feel they are trustworthy; our attachment then gives rise to an even deeper trust. A positive virtuous circle develops between trust and attachment. We all desperately need people we can trust and this helps to explain why people benefit from a strong relationship with God, who is more trustworthy than even the best human being can possibly be. The empathetic support of a spiritual friend can help someone move from distrust to trust.

Our need for trust is summed up beautifully in a poem on Trust by D.H. Lawrence which starts, 'Oh we've got to trust one another again in some essentials'. He longs for something better than 'the narrow little bargaining trust that says: I'm for you if you'll be for me'; and dreams of 'a bigger trust, a trust of the sun' that we can see shining in one another.

*Question:*

*Do you have people you can trust?*

*Can other people trust you?*

## Pastoral Relationships

Pastoral relationships are in some ways like any other relationships, but they also have some special features. Normally, they are a one-way relationship in which one person is there exclusively for the other, giving them complete attention. In most relationships, things move smoothly backwards and forwards, focusing on one person and then the other. There can also be a kind of 'co-counselling' hybrid in which people take it in turns to be focused exclusively on the other.

In a professional counselling relationship there are usually strict boundaries, with one person attending for pastoral care from the other at specific, regular times, and with no other contact. It is one of the distinctive features of pastoral care in church settings that it is often less boundaried and structured. A member of a church community can meet a pastor in a range of different situations, sometimes with brief snatches of one-to-one conversation, and it is often just pastoral conversation rather than formal counselling. There are advantages in the greater naturalness of that way of working, but it is open to abuse. A person in need can start to make unreasonable demands on the pastor, and the pastor can take advantage of the relationship to meet their own needs.

There are often several distinct elements in a pastoral relationship. The first (and the most essential) is that the person should be listened to and feel understood. Some people talk very freely and just need to be given the opportunity; others need more help and encouragement. Either way, it is usually helpful for people not just to express previously rehearsed thoughts, but to go deeper; talking can help them to understand themselves more deeply. Feeling understood by someone else often goes hand in hand with understanding yourself better.

In this listening element of pastoral conversation, it is helpful to borrow some of the elements of the non-directive or person-centred counselling developed by Carl Rogers that we have already mentioned in this chapter. One of the key features is to attend particularly to what the other person is evidently *feeling,* and to reflect that back to them in way that encourages them to go further in putting their feelings into words. The aim is to provide them with the three key conditions that will help them to understand themselves more deeply: accurate empathy, warmth or 'unconditional positive regard', and genuineness. They are conditions that come close to the Christian ideal of love.

Some people prefer to stay with good listening, but it is often helpful to go further, and to offer some sound, common-sense advice. Great care needs to be exercised over advising someone to do something that they do not already see is in their best interests. However, if there is something they already think would be helpful, but are finding it hard to do, it is straightforward to encourage them to actually do it. It can also be useful to help them to think of ways in which they could make it as easy as possible for themselves, such as breaking it down into manageable stages. That can help people to change their behaviour, which will in turn affect how they feel.

It is important for spiritual friends and companions to respect the freedom and autonomy of the other person. They may offer advice, but they should never try to impose it. Sometimes the advice may need to be strong and firm, and it is interesting that most of Jesus' healings are brought about by his giving an order that had to be obeyed, such as telling the lepers to go and show themselves to the priests. We can all become so deeply locked into our egocentricity that it is hard for us to do what is in our best interests without a word of command from someone who has our best interests at heart.

But, however firm the command, and however much it is given in the best interests of the other person, spiritual authority should always be offered and never imposed. It is important to help people to do what they themselves recognise as being in their best interests, and not to try to decide that for them.

Kenneth Leech puts this very clearly in his classic book, *Soul Friend*. The soul friend 'is not a leader, but a guide'. We live in an age in which it seems that the spiritual life must be a path of freedom if it is to work at all. As Leech says, the soul friend has a ministry of liberation, helping people and communities in their journey towards freedom. In the spiritual life, it is helpful for most of us to have a spiritual companion or 'soul friend'. Sometimes people play that role for each other; sometimes the spiritual relationship goes just one way, as with a mentor or pastor. Whichever, it is essential to focus on helping the other person to follow their own spiritual path, not to impose our own.

## Prayer Companions

Finally, in pastoral work, it can also often be helpful to pray together. It is the most distinctive feature of religious or spiritual pastoral care, but it often makes a decisive difference. In my experience it is best not to rush into prayer too quickly, but to start by doing the more obvious things of listening to someone and perhaps giving them practical advice. What is needed after that is something to help the person to actually take a fresh approach, with a new heart and mind.

Sometimes secular counselling lacks any good way of bringing that about; it can prepare the ground but often doesn't know how to clinch things. However, pastoral care in a religious setting has in prayer a very good way of doing that. I don't think it is helpful to worry too much about how prayer works, whether it is human or divine, psychological or spiritual. It is best seen as a human activity conducted with an explicit awareness of the presence of God, and within his guiding providence. It brings the two people together in God's presence; it focuses the mind and heart of each person; it engenders confidence, trust and hope; and it creates the possibility of a fresh approach. All that is enormously helpful in bringing about real change.

Prayer is especially important when one person faces a difficult challenge, one that they are finding it hard to make headway with. It can be very powerful to meet with a spiritual friend, and for both people to pray together about whatever the problem is. Though it is helpful for us to pray on our own, there seems to be a particular power that comes from people meeting together to pray.

Praying together is useful not only in pastoral care; it is also one of the key hallmarks of a spiritual friendship. It transforms a friendship in a remarkable way when people pray or meditate together on a regular basis. It is less important whether that prayer is spoken or silent. What makes a difference is that both people turn to the spiritual centre beyond themselves that we call 'God'. It invites a third presence, a spiritual presence, into a relationship when two people pray together.

When a relationship includes prayer, it can move the entire relationship on to a new plane; everything becomes more spiritually focused. There can be a new shared awareness of the spiritual significance of everything that happens in the relationship. It becomes a friendship in which there is an enhanced awareness of how everything can contribute positively or negatively to the unfolding purposes of God. It can also bring a new energy to the relationship and to everything that arises from it, and a new calm and peace in which everything feels more stable and settled.

Praying together seems to open us up to spiritual resources beyond ourselves, and to unlock the door that leads us out of whatever problem we have become trapped in. Sometimes one person will place their hands on the head of the other person and pray for a blessing on them. Blessing one another, in God's name, can be a powerful part of spiritual friendship.

> *Question:*
>
> *Recall how times when praying with someone has been a powerful experience* or *imagine what that could be like.*

## Bible Study

The Bible is full of stories of relationships. The story of Adam and Eve is the first relationship in the Bible (Genesis 2:4–7 and 15–24). The account of the female being taken from the male may sound strange to modern ears, but the key point seems to be that humans need companions; the man 'clings to his wife and they become one flesh'.

In the Old Testament the story of Joseph's early life (Genesis 37:1–31) illustrates many issues about the formation of attachments. See again Sara Savage (2011) *Joseph: Insights for the Spiritual Journey.* SPCK. Chapter one.

The story of the relationships of Jacob and Esau with their father Isaac, and the troubled sibling rivalry between them (Genesis. 27:10–40) also raises many issues about attachment relationships. There are also many stories of close bonds forming between people, and the story of the covenant that David and Jonathan made with each other (1 Samuel 18:1–5) illustrates the diversity of these close relationships.

There is less about human relationships in the New Testament but, though we lack detail, there are tantalising glimpses into several key relationships of Jesus. Probably the most important one is with his unseen 'heavenly Father'. This comes through most clearly in John's Gospel, where Jesus repeatedly refers to his relationship with the Father, for example in John 10:14–18 and 29–30.

There is also Jesus' enigmatic relationship with his mother. Jesus sometimes seems quite dismissive of his mother (Matthew 12:46–50), but on the cross he shows love and concern for her, and commends her and John to each other (John 19:26–27), John probably being the beloved disciple who was reclining next to him at the Last Supper (John 13–23).

## Background and Sources

There is some helpful basic material about attachments and relationships in Jessica Rose (2013) *Psychology for Pastoral Contexts: A Handbook.* SCM Press. Chapters four and five.

On counselling, see Fraser Watts, Rebecca Nye and Sara Savage (2002) *Psychology for Christian Ministry.* Routledge. Chapter ten 'Counselling and Pastoral Care'.

On the psychology of attachment relationships, see:

Colby Pearce (2016) *A Short Introduction to Attachment and Attachment Disorder.* 2nd Edition. Jessica Kingsley.

David Howe (2011) *Attachment Across the Lifecourse: A Brief Introduction.* Palgrave Macmillan.

The classic book looking at religion through the lens of attachment theory is

Lee A. Kirkpatrick (2004) *Attachment, Evolution, and the Psychology of Religion.* Guilford Press. I have summarised work in his area in Fraser Watts (2017) *Psychology, Religion and Spirituality.* Cambridge University Press. pp. 114–17.

Victor Counted and I have explored place attachment in the Bible in

Victor Counted and Fraser Watts (2017) 'Place Attachment in the Bible: The Role of Attachment to Sacred Places in Religious Life'. *Journal of Psychology and Theology,* vol. 45, pp. 218–32.

A good guide to the person-centred counselling developed by Carl Rogers is

David Mearns, Brian Thorne and Julia McLeod (2013) *Person-Centred Counselling in Action.* Sage. On its relationship to Christianity, see Brian Thorne (2012) *Counselling and Spiritual Accompaniment: Bridging Faith and Person-Centred Therapy.* Wiley-Blackwell.

On prayer relationships see John C. Maxwell (2012) *Partners in Prayer.* Thomas Nelson. On prayer in counselling see Peter Gubi and Brian Thorne (2007) *Prayer in Counselling and Psychotherapy: Exploring a Hidden Meaningful Dimension.* Jessica Kingsley.

# Chapter Seven
## *Community*

## Living in Groups

Humans need groups, as well as one-to-one relationships. Some people naturally gravitate mainly to one-to-one relationships, while others prefer groups. That just reflects differences between people, and there is no right or wrong about it. However, we all need to belong to groups to some degree; and belonging to a group raises special issues.

Humans seem to form different kinds of groups from other primates. There are strong links, for example, within a pack of hunting dogs, where the key issues seem to be about how well a particular dog is accepted within the pack, and the relative status of the various dogs in the pack. Humans seem to have gone further in allowing individuality and autonomy within a group. At our best, we can accept individuality, and even encourage it, while still maintaining strong social bonds.

One of the key issues is how to maintain those group bonds. Many primates groom each other as a way of ensuring that a group hangs together. That seems to work well, but it is very time-consuming. Humans seem to have evolved less time-consuming ways of maintaining social groups, and some experts such as Robin Dunbar think that religion played an important role in that for early humans.

Religion seems to have started from group activities, and with what people *did* together. Religious *thinking* came later. The earliest form of religion was probably people dancing together around the campfire. The way people move together makes a big difference; it needs to be rhythmic and it needs to be synchronised. When a group of people do that together, it has a remarkable effect on their sense of being a group; it triggers bodily processes (especially endorphins) that enabled early humans to bond together in much larger numbers than was possible for other similar creatures. That was good for co-operation and, therefore, good for survival. The march of the Israelites around Jericho (Joshua 6:1–20) has many of the hallmarks of an early religious ritual, and would have had powerful effects on those involved at many levels, biological, social and spiritual.

It was also the soil from which religion arose. Dancing still plays a role in some forms of religion, especially in Pentecostal and charismatic forms of Christianity. Dancing bonds people together and can give them a 'high' that expands consciousness, allowing them to enter a spiritual world in which they are in contact with angels, devils and ancestral spirits. Because this expanded consciousness arose from dancing in which everyone had participated, they all entered this spiritual world together; it was part of their collective experience.

A little later, as people started to make sense of these group experiences, storytelling played an important role. Religion started with experience, not with theology, and religious thinking started with stories before it moved on to abstract doctrines. Stories have always played a key role in religion and in bonding people, and I will come back to them at the end of this chapter. Laughing with other people also plays an important role in bonding people together and engenders a sense of joy.

How groups operate depends on how big they are. Small groups of up to about a dozen people can be quite close. Jesus chose a group of disciples of that size to support him in his ministry. It was one of the first things he did at the start of his public work. They ate and slept together, and shared everything.

Many churches have come to realise that it helps people to grow in their spiritual life to belong to a small group meeting in someone's home, as well as to a larger congregation. Even in a small group there can be enough people to offer a rich variety of resources to meet particular needs. It is only in the last fifty years that home groups have become a standard part of religious life, and it has been a very helpful development.

At the other end of the spectrum, there is probably a special intensity that is achieved with very large groups. This can be used for good or ill. Nazi Germany became very skilful at using large rallies to bond the German nation together, and Adolf Hitler became very effective in addressing them. Somewhat similar processes seem to operate in large religious rallies, where people can surrender themselves to the speaker and to the crowd; it can be a very intense group experience.

As groups get larger, they inevitably become less intimate, though there are some things that can be done better by a larger group of people. Between the home group and the large rally there are various in-between groups that seem to be a kind of compromise, small enough for people still to be able to network, rather than just become absorbed in the crowd, but large enough to be uplifting and inspiring.

At various points you seem to reach a kind of ceiling. In the kind of church or group where everyone networks, you seem to reach a ceiling at about fifty; it is what has been called a 'family size' church. You seem to reach another ceiling at about 150, what has been called a 'pastoral size' church. It seems hard for us to maintain connection with the various members of a group larger than that, and no pastor can connect directly with more people than that. Around 150 is probably roughly the number of the hunter-gatherer groups that used dance to bond together.

These different group processes are reflected in the way churches grow. As churches grow they often hit a ceiling. To continue to grow, churches need to find different ways of organising themselves, and often operate for many purposes as a set of loosely connected subgroups.

*Question:*
*What does it feel like to be part of a group of like-minded people?*

## Marks of Group Membership

Human groups always have badges of membership; things that are expected of people if they are to be accepted as a full member of the group. Churches are no exception, though it is equally true of any other kind of group.

Body posture is often important in churches, for example. It is not just that you have to stand, sit or kneel at the right times; it is often more subtle than that. Ways of speaking (or praying) are often crucial to the identity of a church. People have strong feelings about prayers being set or extempore, about whether they are in traditional or modern language, about forms of intercession, and much more. If you join a church it is crucial to learn how to speak if you want to be accepted as a full member.

Churches differ in what is required, making it hard to get it right. For example, in some churches it is common to put a hand in the air when standing to sing a hymn; in other churches it is definitely *not* acceptable to do that. You have to know the implicit membership rules in order to fit in. Some churches like to think that they are very friendly and informal, and don't mind about any of these things. But, even in informal churches, there are often particular ways of being informal that are expected of people who really want to belong.

There is a good and a bad side to all this. The good side is that having clear marks of membership helps people to feel they belong. It strengthens the bonds that hold people together. It gives a group a strong sense of identity. That makes the group more attractive to potential members, and more effective in getting things done.

But there are downsides. One is that it makes the group more difficult to join. It is unsettling to join a group where there are a lot of rules that you need to know in order to really belong, but which are unstated and no one tells you about. The other big downside is that having implicit marks of membership imposes conformity on everyone. The assumption is that this is what 'we' do, and that if you are really 'one of us', you will do this too. That can stifle individuality and creativity. It can also make groups such as churches rather static and leave them stuck in a rut, in what looks to an outsider like a time warp.

Pressures to conform to group norms can be very strong, and there has been a good deal of research investigating this. It depends on various things such as how large the group is, how important the group is to you, how much a particular individual wants to be liked and valued in the group, how expert or authoritative other people in the group are perceived to be, and whether there are any dissenters in the group.

Religion may be especially vulnerable to pressures to conformity. Religious judgements are generally not about things that are blindingly obvious; they can always be argued either way. That makes it hard for one person to stand out against the crowd. The other issue is that religion is so important to people. Religious issues are often seen as 'matters of principle' that are really important, which makes it hard to be a dissenter, at least within a group that one is closely identified with. People who can normally see different points of view can switch into being 'black and white' when it comes to religion, or other matters of principle.

It is very different, of course, if two groups are taking different and opposite views on a religious issue. That just increases the pressure to conformity, as the need to be different from the other group is added to the need to be in agreement with your own group. Religion actually seems unusually vulnerable to splitting into different groups with opposing views. The pressures to conformity within a group are unusually strong, but the tendency to split into opposing views is also strong.

There are ways of combatting the pull towards excessive conformity. It helps for groups such as churches to recognise their implicit membership requirements, which are often much more extensive and demanding than they realise. It also helps if churches encourage people to be counter-cultural, and to do innovative things. Gradually, the dead-hand conformity can be lifted, through honesty and creativity. The key is to recognise and celebrate diversity.

These are age-old issues. In the New Testament, as we have seen, St Paul had to point out to Christians at Corinth that it takes people with many different gifts to build a church, and that people need to be allowed to be themselves, and to exercise whatever different gifts they have. It is no good expecting everyone to be the same. As St Paul says, expecting everyone to make the same contribution makes no more sense than expecting all the parts of the body to be the same; as he says, a body that is composed entirely of eyes, or of ears would be of no use. It helps that we are different from one another, and can each play to our strengths, and compensate for each other's weaknesses.

> *Question:*
> *Think of a church or other group you know and try to see what the implicit marks of membership are.*

## Individualism, Conformity and Interdependence

We often struggle over having rather mixed attitudes to relationships. We partly want to be close to each other and we long for intimacy. However, we also want to be separate, to be ourselves, and not to be swallowed up into other people. It is one of the great challenges of our time to find a way in which people can be themselves, but still have a strong sense of belonging.

These days, most people are determined to be themselves. As we already noted, integrity, authenticity and genuineness are important virtues in our time. Everyone's goal is to discover their true nature and identity, and to make a reality of that. As many have said, we live in an age of extraordinary individualism. People still adopt strong identities and loyalties, so individualism has its limitations. But at least the values and rhetoric of our time are about being true to yourself.

Individualism is not all bad. Cast in a religious way, it reflects traditional values; in trying to discover our unique nature, we may be searching for the people God made us to be. We are all different, so becoming what we are called to be is something unique and individual. Christians have long been encouraged to try to discern their own particular vocation, and to follow that. Discerning who you really are is much like finding out what you are really called to do.

But alongside all this individualism, we have seen extraordinarily powerful mass movements in the last hundred years, including forms of communism, fascism and even religious extremism, that completely take people over. Some of these mass movements are atheistic, but some are religious. They can take either form.

There is something intoxicating about being part of a group with such a strong identity that it suppresses all individuality. Becoming a suicide bomber is the ultimate in the individual being taken over by a group cause; but there can be no doubt about the appeal that it has for many people today. Despite the talk about being your true self, many people seem eager to surrender themselves to a bigger cause.

There are no easy answers to this, but it is possible to offer some pointers, drawing in part on the Christian tradition.

Firstly, it helps to remember that the people we are dealing with, whatever the context, are humans, like ourselves. One of the things that goes wrong when people start exploiting one another is that they 'dehumanise' the people they are dealing with and suspend all empathy with them. They treat them just as cogs in a machine. Jesus talked about the importance of being good neighbours, as in the story of the Good Samaritan; neighbourliness is an important social virtue with a long religious history.

Catholic social teaching has also laid a strong emphasis on the dignity of every human person, and understands the value of keeping social structures on a scale where we can't ignore the fact that we are dealing with other human beings. We can try to maintain the human scale of interaction as best we can, and to look for structures where we can do business with people we know, and whom we can treat as neighbours.

Failing to treat other people with appropriate dignity is especially pronounced in war, where people on the other side are treated just as enemies to be killed; all thoughts of their personality, family and friends are put aside. Sometimes, when war is over, people who were on opposite sides meet each other as human beings and feel regret that they tried to kill each other. There is a poignant line in Wilfred Owen's war poem, *Strange Meeting,* when one dead man says to another who had been on the opposite side, 'I am the enemy you killed, my friend.'

Secondly, we can raise our consciousness to become increasingly aware of how dependent on one another we actually are. There is a dangerous current trend in politics for social groupings to want to pretend that they are more self-sufficient than they actually are. That leads to separatist movements in which countries, or parts of countries, believe that they can function perfectly well on their own. The wish to believe this is so strong that it leads people to turn a blind eye to economic realities. The same separatist spirit leads people to ignore the contribution made by immigrants to their prosperity.

We have a growing sense of the complex 'ecology' in the natural world, in which species depend on one another in a great variety of ways. No species could exist on its own; every species is dependent on numerous other species for its survival. We need a similar sense of interdependence in human life too, and reflection on the world of nature might help us to see that.

We seem to be subject to two conflicting forces, both of which are very strong. On the one hand, the economic order is becoming increasingly interconnected, and we are dependent on each other for our mutual prosperity and flourishing. On the other hand, there is a deep yearning to identify with people of our own kind. Humanity urgently needs to find ways of harmonising this yearning for a specific social and cultural identity with the realities of economic interdependence.

Thirdly, it helps for humanity to have a sense of the spiritual centre around which we all revolve, whether or not we name it as 'God'. There are many different beliefs about that spiritual centre, and many different words for it. However, the vast majority of humans have some such belief, and it would help to rebuild healthy forms of community across the globe to realise that it is something most people have in common.

There has been an idea around in the West for some decades now that the world was becoming more secular, and that the best way for people of different faiths to get along was for us all to adopt secularism as a neutral meeting ground. However, it is surely now clear, for better or worse, that the idea that we are moving towards secularism is mistaken. The vast majority of the world's population remain deeply religious in one way or another, and there is no prospect of that changing. Moreover, the distrust of secularism among many religious people is even deeper than the distrust of people of other faiths. The future of humanity seems to lie, not in secularism, but in a spiritual pluralism, in which most people acknowledge, in one way or another, some kind of spiritual centre.

There will need to be a place within this family of spiritualities for those who see themselves as more spiritual than religious. There are now many people in the West who have that approach. Their spirituality may be largely a rather individualistic 'self-spirituality', but I believe it is largely derived from more conventional religions, especially Christianity and Buddhism. Despite its divergence from them, it has many things in common with them.

> *Question:*
> *How can we be ourselves but also be close to others?*

## Telling Our Story

A key factor that holds people together is a sense of having a common story to tell. It is very important in many social movements. Jews, Christians and other religious groups also have their own particular stories to tell. So do some non-religious groups such as Marxists.

Having a common story comes over very strongly in the Old Testament. The Jewish people whose story is told there had a very strong sense of being the people whom God had delivered from slavery in Egypt, brought through the Red Sea, and led through the desert to the Promised Land. When you read the Old Testament you get the feeling that every Israelite felt they were part of that story.

Christians have a similar sense of being part of a common story, being the people formed by the death and Resurrection of Jesus, people with a common mission to continue the task of building what Jesus called his 'kingdom', people who gather to share bread and wine in Jesus' name, people commanded to take the message of repentance (*metanoia*, a new heart and mind) and forgiveness to people everywhere.

Having a common story is generally a healthy way of establishing a common purpose. It does not require the surrender of individual identity that can be seen in some mass rallies. It also does not require that everyone conforms to the same template, with a complete elimination of individuality. People need to identify with the same collective story rather than showing the same marks of group membership. It is an approach that leaves people more freedom.

For various reasons there has probably been a weakening in the sense of having a common identity in countries such as Britain. Having a shared religious faith contributes to that sense of identity, but there is no faith that is now shared by enough people in Britain to serve that purpose. Being invaded contributes to the sense of identity of a country, and few people can now remember Britain being invaded.

However, a common identity can arise at a more local level too. Sometimes religious people in a particular place, with common beliefs, develop a common story about their situation and identity. One inspiring example that I have already referred to is the congregation of Coventry Cathedral who developed a strong sense of being the people whose cathedral was bombed in World War II and then rebuilt. They saw it as their task to work for reconciliation, first between Britain and Germany, and then to the ends of the earth.

The cathedral was led for the forty years after the bombing by two long-serving, single-minded and visionary leaders – Dick Howard and Bill Williams – with very similar understandings of the cathedral's mission and role in the world. Howard saw a close identity between the ruined and rebuilt cathedral and the death and

Resurrection of Christ. He saw the central role of forgiveness and had the words of Jesus – 'Father Forgive' – carved on the east wall of the cathedral, behind the altar. In a memorable Christmas broadcast made just weeks after the bombing, he said, 'We are going to try to make a kinder, simpler, a more Christ-childlike sort of world in the days beyond this strife.'

Williams framed that mission in terms of 'reconciliation', the word with which the cathedral is now most closely identified. As you drive into Coventry, you see on the road signs that Coventry is a 'city of peace and reconciliation'; the cathedral came to have such a strong identity as a place of reconciliation that it became the identity of the whole city. They took to heart the text in 2 Corinthians where St Paul says, 'In Christ, God was reconciling the world to Himself . . . and He has committed the message of reconciliation to us' (5:19).

People often have their own individual stories to tell too, about who they are, what gifts they have been given, how they have been called to use them, and what they have done well and badly in living out that sense of vocation and identity. The sense of identity we have as individuals, and as members of groups of increasing size, are all nested within each other.

> *Question:*
>
> *Take a church or group you belong to and see what their story is about, who they are and why they matter. If you start with, 'We are the people who . . . how would you go on?*

## Bible Study

Read the story of the Battle of Jericho (Joshua 6:1–20) and imagine as vividly as you can being one of the people involved. Feel the tramp of feet marching together, and the horns blowing, and sense the energy that would have created.

Read about the lifestyle of the first followers of Jesus (Acts 2:43–47) and sense the remarkable solidarity of that group of people. Also read what St Paul says (1 Corinthians 12) about the place of different individual gifts within the same community. Think over how there can be both recognition of the differences between people, but also solidarity between them.

St Paul has a powerful vision of how all those who live in Christ are united together, making all other human divisions irrelevant in comparison (Galatians 3:27–29). Going still further, he sees as a centre of unity for all things in Creation, the one in whom all things cohere (Colossians 1:15–20).

## Background and Sources

On the role of religion in human evolution and social bonding see Robin Dunbar (2014) *Human Evolution: A Pelican Introduction.* Pelican. On church size theory see Alice Mann (1998) *The In-Between Church: Navigating Size Transitions in Congregations.* Rowman & Littlefield Publishers.

For a classic introduction to group processes see Roger Brown (1988) *Group Processes.* Blackwell. On issues of identity and conformity in churches and other groups see Fraser Watts, Rebecca Nye and Sara Savage (2002). *Psychology for Christian Ministry.* Routledge. Chapter eleven 'Social processes in church life'.

Sara Savage and Eolene Boyd-Macmillan (2011) *The Human Face of Church: A Social Psychology and Pastoral Resource for Pioneer and Traditional Ministry.* Canterbury Press.

See also Bruce Reed (1978) *The Dynamics of Religion: Process and Movement in Christian Churches.* Darton, Longman & Todd. Also William Meissner (1966) *Group Dynamics in the Religious Life.* University of Notre Dame Press.

For a Christian view of issues of interdependence and response to a spiritual centre see Stephen Verney (1976) *Into the New Age.* Collins. It is very good on issues of interdependence and response to a spiritual centre.

On the story of Coventry Cathedral as an example of narrative identity, see Christopher A. Lamb (2011) *Reconciling People: Coventry Cathedral's Story.* Canterbury Press (especially chapter six 'The Archangel Michael Takes Wings').

# Chapter Eight
## *Forgiveness and Reconciliation*

## What is Forgiveness?

Forgiveness is at the heart of Christianity. It is not an optional extra for Christians; forgiveness is what Christianity is all about. Jesus insists on forgiveness. He says bluntly in the Sermon on the Mount that, 'If you forgive others their trespasses, your heavenly Father will also forgive you, but if you do not forgive others, neither will your Father forgive your trespasses (Matthew 6:14–15). Clearly, someone who is not prepared to forgive can't claim to be a Christian. At the end of Luke's Gospel, Jesus gives his disciples a charge to preach 'repentance and forgiveness of sins' to all nations (Luke 24:40). The gospel they are to spread is the gospel of forgiveness.

Forgiveness is both what *God* does and what *we* do. It is both, and the two are linked. The Lord's Prayer makes that clear: 'Forgive us our sins, as we forgive those who sin against us.' God may have started the dance of forgiveness, but it is a dance we are invited to join in. The forgiveness of God and human forgiveness work together; they are more transformative together than either is alone.

Both 'repentance' and 'forgiveness' are widely misunderstood. For most people they have very negative connotations. So does the word 'sin', which we will look at in a later chapter. But I am convinced that for Jesus and those who wrote the New Testament, all three words were primarily words of promise and hope.

We have already noted that 'repentance' is a translation of the Greek word *metanoia*, which means having a new heart and mind. That sounds much more positive and constructive than 'repentance'. It is primarily about the personal transformation that is needed if we are to stop messing things up for ourselves and other people.

To achieve that new heart and mind, there will certainly need to be an honest recognition of what we have done wrong, and the harm it has done to others, and sometimes to ourselves too. That involves peeling back the layers of self-deception and self-justification from which we all suffer, and learning to see things straight. It is about a radical change of direction, a turning again, about seeing things clearly, and then taking appropriate corrective action.

I feel that 'repentance' is such a misleading translation of this key concept in Jesus' thinking that it might be best to abandon it altogether and try a different word. 'Renewal' or 'return' or 'turning again' come closer. It is about returning to being right with God, right with the cosmos, right with how things were meant to be, right with ourselves.

'Forgiveness' is also a bad translation; the New Testament word is usually *aphesis,* and again 'forgiveness' sounds too gloomy. It sounds as though we are being let off our punishment for some wrongdoing. Jesus means much more than that; he is talking about a more comprehensive 'release' or 'letting go', letting go of a rope that has become taut or letting go of prisoners. It also evokes a picture of letting go at the start of a race. Imagine a set of competitors lined up to run a race. The race is started, and they are released, set free for the race. If forgiveness does its job, it releases us; it sets us free.

Scholars have recognised that 'forgiveness' is very difficult to define, and there is no agreed definition. It is different from condoning, excusing, forgetting or pardoning, but it is hard to say exactly what it is. Part of the problem is that forgiveness, at its best, involves something inside us *and* something between us and another person. It is not just one or the other, but involves a conjunction of these two elements.

Also, interestingly, it is often easier to say what forgiveness brings to an end than what it starts. It is easier to define what it replaces. Forgiveness brings an end to negative feelings such as guilt, anger and resentment. It brings 'release' from such things; it involves 'letting go' of all the negative feelings that we may have carried within us. This idea of 'letting go' brings us very close to what the New Testament means by forgiveness. Things are restored to their original state, to how they are meant to be. In this, the real meanings of 'repentance' and 'forgiveness' are very close.

But there is a positive, forward-looking element to forgiveness as well. Forgiveness creates opportunities that we are freed up to explore. One Christian thinker, Werner Pelz, said that forgiveness is a 'creative endeavour to bring into existence new conditions and situations for an intenser and profounder exploration of our common human heritage' (p. 139). Forgiveness liberates us for all sorts of possibilities.

So, if we translate what Jesus tells his followers to preach as repentance and forgiveness of sins, I don't think that really captures all that he meant. I think the message that he wants his followers to preach is one of renewal and release. That is at the heart of the new way of living he called his 'kingdom'.

> *Question:*
>
> *What do you understand by 'forgiveness'?*
>
> *Has reading this section changed what it means for you?*

## From Guilt to Forgiveness

One of the things that forgiveness releases us from is guilt. It is not all that forgiveness releases us from; it also releases us from anger and resentment, and much else. Different people need release from different things, and forgiveness is a tool in the Christian armoury with a wide range of benefits. But release from guilt is among them and, sadly, there are all too many people wracked with guilt. Let us see how that works, how people can get from the burden of guilt created by wrongdoing to the release that comes with forgiveness.

Many people are troubled by guilt, but it is important to ascertain whether or not someone is right to feel guilty. On the one hand there is realistic guilt, which is an appropriate response to what someone has done wrong. However, there is also neurotic guilt, which is an excessive and disproportionate response to wrongdoing. Sometimes guilt is not appropriate at all, as people can feel guilty when, by any objective standards, they have done nothing wrong at all. Neurotic and realistic guilt need handling in different ways.

Appropriate guilt needs to be acknowledged, and the path to release depends on that open acknowledgement. We need, first, to acknowledge our guilt ourselves; there is no way out of it unless we do so. But it is important to admit it to others, to admit it to at least one other human person and, for those who have a spiritual life, also admit it in the presence of God. Bringing another person into the picture helps to give us some objectivity; it helps to ensure that the admission of wrongdoing is real; it also helps us to move on from the guilt and to take on board the release from guilt that forgiveness involves.

In some Christian circles, the admission of guilt would be to a priest and would take the form of confession. That can be helpful; it is one of the most moving and humbling aspects of the work of a priest to hear the confession of someone who is wracked with guilt, and to help them to feel the deep relief that comes with forgiveness. However, something comparable can happen without a priest and outside a church setting, and the overuse of formal confession can increase people's sense of guilt rather than bringing them release from it.

When we were looking generally at relationships in chapter six, we noted that important relationships, such as parenting, often combine two strands. One involves judgement and the setting of boundaries; the other involves love and nurture. This combination is present in forgiveness. There is no shrinking from what has been done wrong; that is admitted with clarity and honesty. However, it is combined with a warm positive regard for the person who has done wrong that helps them to move on.

The tendency to feel excessive, neurotic guilt is a very different problem, and needs a different approach. It is again helpful to involve another person, who can bring some objectivity to whether or not any serious wrongdoing has been committed, and help the person to find a way out of their excessive scrupulosity. That often arises, not from any great concern for the welfare of others, but rather from an excessive self-absorption.

Neurotic guilt often arises from a deep-seated sense of inadequacy, and involves a distorted perception of the harm we imagine we have caused. Sometimes people who are burdened by neurotic guilt have a deep sense of shame about the kind of person they are, even when they have not actually done much wrong. Guilt focuses on what we have done, but when guilt becomes pervasive it can often arise from shame about ourselves.

There seems to be a kind of oscillation through history between being focused mainly on guilt about what we have done and shame about who we are. Our present age is not as concerned with guilt about wrongdoing as some others have been; perhaps not as much as it should be. However, many people seem troubled by a deep sense of shame and inadequacy, about not being as good as other people (not as nice, not as successful, or whatever). They are troubled more by what they have failed to do, as by any wrongdoing that they have actually done.

In confession and forgiveness, Christians have a good way of releasing people from guilt about what they have done. However, they do not seem to have developed any comparable way of helping people with a deep-seated sense of shame about who they are. What they need to know is that God loves them and accepts them as they are. That can do a lot to alleviate their deep sense of shame and inadequacy. The practical question is how best to convey to people that they are loved and accepted, regardless of what they may have done or failed to do.

*Question:*
*How far are your guilt feelings realistic?*
*How far are they excessive?*

## From Division to Reconciliation

Now we will look at how forgiveness can move us from division in society to reconciliation; let us now see how that works. Society is full of division now, just as it was in Jesus' time. St Paul talks about the divisions between Jew and Greek, slave and free, male and female (Galatians 3:28). Looking at our own society we can add the divisions between rich and poor, and between weak and powerful, divisions between immigrants and indigenous members of society, between people of different faiths, between humans and other animals etc. As society gets more complex, there is ever more scope for division. Had St Paul been writing now, he would probably have included many of those in his list too. In a sense, the divisions he does mention stand for all human divisions.

St Paul's bold claim is that all these various divisions are overcome in Christ, that in Christ *all* are united. Christ is above all a reconciler. Christ, he claims, reconciles humanity and God, and brings reconciliation wherever there is division within humanity or within Creation. Reconciliation is what Christ is for, what he is about, what he does. In the Sermon on the Mount, Jesus tells a simple story about the importance he attaches to reconciliation. Someone whose sister or brother had a grievance against him goes to make a sacrifice at the altar. Jesus says, 'leave your gift there before the altar and go: first be reconciled to your brother or sister and then come and offer your gift' (Matthew 5:23–4).

How does reconciliation come about, and what is the role of forgiveness? A key insight is that when there are divisions there are no winners. The idea that you can 'win' a war is a misleading fantasy; in reality, wars are never really won. War should be seen as a deep sickness in society, in which all concerned are victims. The winners usually sustain deep casualties of many kinds that are often only slightly less grievous than those of the so-called losers. In reality, where there is division and war, we are all losers. Many judged that World War II was unavoidable, but no one came out of it better off; all suffered.

Divisions are only overcome when all concerned recognise that they are victims, when they repent of their divisions and seek healing and reconciliation. First of all, we all need to recognise our need for forgiveness for our own divisive and oppositional conduct. Forgiveness that goes only one way can end up being experienced as patronising. Forgiveness needs to be mutual; it needs to be both given and received.

Reconciliation becomes more complex when it is between groups, not just between individuals. It is necessary for people to actually get to know each other and to rebuild trust, to realise that people on the other side are much like us. It can also call for big gestures that catch the imagination, such as when the people of the bombed and rebuilt cathedral in Coventry rebuilt a hospital in Dresden, one of the German towns most heavily bombed by Britain. The international network of partners in reconciliation that has grown up around Coventry has been built around three core principles that have wide application, and deserve careful consideration.

Firstly, there is 'healing the wounds of history'. Many deep-seated conflicts are kept alive by historical events, which are often commemorated annually and kept alive as part of the shared identity of a community. Particular problems arise when the memory of those historical events keeps resentments alive against a neighbouring community. People sometimes seem determined never to forget. In such circumstances, there needs to be mutual forgiveness before there can be healing of the shadow cast by historical events. It is important to enter into the different narrative of the other community, and to understand how the same event can look very different from opposite sides of the fence.

The second principle is 'learning to live with difference and celebrate diversity'. People are different from one another; equally, communities are very different from one another. There is a strong human tendency to bond with people like ourselves, people who share our history and identity, perhaps also (as sociobiologists would argue) people whose genes are similar to our own. As the trend towards global interaction becomes stronger, the pull towards local identities (and separatism) becomes stronger. That is a natural and understandable reaction, but it helps enormously in the path towards reconciliation if we are able to accept diversity and find things to like in people with different backgrounds.

Thirdly, there is a need to 'build a culture of peace'. Wars are so common that they become the standard pattern; people get so used to wars that they accept them as a matter of course. The majority of Christians reluctantly accept that there are exceptional circumstances in which war becomes necessary, though there is also a strong tradition of Christian pacifism. But war too easily becomes the norm rather than the exception. We need to build a stronger culture of resolving problems in other ways, and forgiveness plays a key role in that.

> *Question:*
> *How far are your guilt feelings realistic?*
> *How far are they excessive?*

## How to Forgive

As we have seen, it is easiest to define forgiveness in terms of what we let go when we forgive; it brings an end to resentment, anger and other similar negative feelings. We are better off when we free ourselves up from such things, so it is not surprising that we feel the benefit when we forgive. But how do we go about forgiveness? That is where psychology comes in. Religion has taught us the importance of forgiveness, but psychology may be better at showing us how to actually go about it.

One aspect of forgiveness is 'reframing', or learning to look at things differently.

There is much religious wisdom about forgiveness that says similar things. For example, Bishop Butler, a distinguished Irish Church leader and philosopher of the eighteenth century, talks in a sermon about how it helps to place yourself 'at a distance', and to learn to see the wrongdoing as arising from 'inadventure or mistake', rather from 'malice or scorn'. That is reframing by another name.

One of the best-known psychological approaches to forgiveness comes from Professor Everett Worthington, who came to forgiveness the hard way, as a result of his mother being murdered by a burglar. That led to a very intense exploration of forgiveness in which he was engaged both personally and as a psychologist. Worthington sees forgiveness as involving five specific stages. He suggests that, as we work through these stages, we have someone in mind that we are finding it hard to forgive.

The first stage is to recall the 'offence' that we are finding it hard to forgive. He suggests that, while we are learning to forgive, it is best not to choose someone where the offence is great and where the wound is still fresh; it is also best initially to choose someone with whom we are not currently in contact, else they may do something to cause fresh upset. However, we do really need to engage with the sense of offence if we are to transform it. There is a parallel here with what we said about needing to really engage with grief, if we are to work through that.

Next we need to empathise with the person who has offended us, to learn to see the world as they see it, and feel what they feel. When we are offended at how someone has behaved, we naturally tend to see things in a rather egocentric way, which makes forgiveness very difficult; so we may need to really work at imagining how the offence looked from the point of view of the other person. It may help to write a letter as though you were the person who has offended you, to help you to get inside their point of view.

Next, it helps to work on our humility. Again there is a vicious circle. Feeling that someone has offended us makes us self-righteous and proud, and that lack of humility entrenches us in our lack of forgiveness. It helps to recall times when we have been no better than the person who has offended us. Gratitude helps too; we can recall times when we have been forgiven and have been grateful for it.

Only when people have done all that prior work are they ready to actually forgive. It is essential to do the psychological groundwork before imagining that we can forgive someone. If we try to forgive prematurely, it won't go deep and it won't stick. However, even then, there is the challenge of holding on to forgiveness when resentment and unforgiveness begin to reassert themselves again. We should be prepared for that, and expect to have to work at holding on to our hard-won decision to forgive.

That is all internal work but, if the person who has offended us is still alive and we are in still in touch with them, there is the separate task of trying to achieve reconciliation with them. Again, Everett Worthington is helpful in setting out the steps that we need to go through. It begins, of course, with the decision to seek reconciliation, and deciding when and how to go about that.

Even if we have done enough internal work to be ready to forgive, we may find that there is further work we need to do in softening our attitudes before we can achieve reconciliation. Resuming contact with the other person may set us back in the inner progress we thought we had made. We may be willing to extend forgiveness to the other person, but may still be too proud to receive it from them.

Toxic feelings may have built up through a period of estrangement, leaving us with a lot of work to do to detoxify ourselves and the relationship. There will also be some positive rebuilding to do, not just dealing with negative feelings but building up positive ones. It helps to become aware of what we have lost through our lack of forgiveness, and to rebuild affection for the other person.

Making the effort to forgive brings people closer to God, even if they don't always realise that. Forgiveness seems to connect people with God, whatever they believe. Forgiveness and reconciliation are at the heart of God's purposes for humanity.

*Question:*
*Take a situation where forgiveness has been hard for you*
*and try applying the approach set out here.*

## Expanding the Horizons of Forgiveness

There is much practical help to be had from the psychological approach to forgiveness which we looked at in the last section, but the religious approach to forgiveness is in some ways broader and deeper. I don't think there is any incompatibility between the two approaches; in fact, I think they can enrich each other. Learning to forgive is not just a matter of handling some specific thing we have found offensive. It is a lifelong journey to become a forgiving person; it is a virtue, a 'pearl of great value' (Matthew 13:45), that we need to work towards over a long period of time. Learning to forgive can be quite demanding.

Religious people see forgiveness as passing on something that has been given to them; not as being all their own initiative. The psychology of forgiveness tends to be individualistic; it focuses on individual people making a personal decision to forgive a specific person for some specific thing they have done. Religious thinking puts individual acts of forgiveness in a broader context. Forgiveness is seen as 'transpersonal', bigger than the individual. The sense that there is a lot of other forgiveness going on can make it easier to undertake a particular act of forgiveness.

Psychology has so far focused primarily on extending forgiveness to others.

However, extending forgiveness to others is intertwined with receiving it ourselves. Receiving forgiveness can be almost as challenging as extending it to others, because it requires humility. When people forgive us, it is easy to react by thinking, 'Who do they think they are, to be doing that?' Forgiveness can sometimes feel patronising, even when it is well intentioned. We don't always want to be forgiven.

We often need people to recognise their faults before we can forgive them, but Jesus doesn't set that as a requirement. With the man lowered through the roof, or the adulterous woman, he doesn't stop to check how sorry they are before extending forgiveness. Even on the cross he sets an example of forgiveness by saying to all concerned, 'Father forgive them, they do not know what they are doing.' There are no preconditions.

Psychology tends to focus on the practical benefits of forgiving, but religion says that forgiveness is just good and right, regardless of the practical advantages. It also emphasises the spiritual benefits of forgiveness. We become better, deeper, people for rising to the challenge of forgiveness. The harder forgiveness is, the more spiritual good it does us.

It helps us to forgive if we learn to see both sides of a question. If we see things in a very black-and-white way, it will be hard for us to make the leap of imagination to see the world as someone else sees it, and especially to see ourselves as others see us. We can't really forgive someone until we understand where the other person is coming from.

In the spiritual life, if it goes well, we learn to rise above our own limited egocentric perspective. There is also a God's-eye view to be taken into account; or, if you prefer, the question of how things look from an ultimate spiritual perspective. The spiritual life has the potential to liberate us from our egocentricity; that can help us with seeing someone else's point of view, and hence with forgiveness.

It also helps with forgiveness if we can rise above black-and-white thinking. Here, it has to be admitted, the impact of religion is mixed. Though religion, or at least Christianity, encourages forgiveness, it can also foster the kind of black-and-white thinking that makes forgiveness very difficult. However, as we will see in chapter ten, some forms of religion can foster the insight that good and evil are intertwined. If they do, it will help with forgiveness.

Forgiveness brings us back into contact with the basic values that underpin Creation, and which flow from the Creator. It is no wonder that forgiveness does us good and makes us feel better.

*Question:*

*Why is forgiveness sometimes so hard to offer?*

## Bible Study

The drought in the Joseph story (Genesis 41:56–43:14) is an interesting case study in forgiveness and unforgiveness [see Sara Savage (2011) *Joseph: Insights for the Spiritual Journey*. SPCK. Chapter four].

Jesus is clear about the importance of forgiveness (Matthew 18:21–35) and reconciliation (Matthew 5:23–24). He has a total understanding of what is involved in forgiveness, as is evident in his saying to the paralytic man (Mark 2:1–12) that it is virtually equivalent to say to forgive the man his sins or to tell him to get up and walk (verse 9).

Jesus sets a moving example of forgiveness from the cross (Luke 23:32–34) in his dealings with the prisoners crucified with him, and in his moving words 'Father Forgive'. His commission to his disciples is to proclaim the gospel of repentance and forgiveness to all people (Luke 24:45–47).

St Paul, in 2 Corinthians 5:17–21, has a powerful vision of reconciliation as being both what God did in Christ, and what we are called to do now.

## Background and Sources

The most helpful book for further reading in this area is Everett L. Worthington Jr. (2003) *Forgiving and Reconciling: Bridges to Wholeness and Hope*. Inter-Varsity Press. An earlier book many found helpful was Lewis Smedes (1988) *Forgive and Forget: Healing the Hurts We Don't Deserve*. Harper & Row.

On rethinking what Christians mean by 'forgiveness' and 'repentance' see Stephen Verney (1989) *The Dance of Love*. Collins.

On problems of guilt see Will van der Hart and Rob Waller (2014) *The Guilt Book: A Path to Grace and Freedom*. Inter-Varsity Press. They combine pastoral and psychological perspectives.

I have brought various perspectives on forgiveness together in Fraser Watts and Liz Gulliford (ed.) (2004) *Forgiveness in Context: Theology and Psychology in Creative Dialogue*. T&T Clark.

On reconciliation in wider society see Russ Parker (2012) *Healing Wounded History*. SPCK.

# Section Three
*Going Deeper*

# Chapter Nine
## *Something More*

The spiritual journey is both a journey within and a journey that transforms our relationships. It is also a journey that includes a growing intuition that there is something more than the human individual. It is to that intuition that I turn now.

## Is There Something More?

In our increasingly post-Christian society, belief in God is no longer obvious. People don't even quite know what it means to 'believe in God'. Some of those who 'believe in God' would struggle to explain what they meant by that. Equally, many atheists have a simplistic idea of the God in whom they don't believe.

I have increasingly come to think that belief in God should be seen as the end point of a journey of spiritual enquiry (even though, in another sense, it is obviously the starting point of a spiritual journey). In this chapter I want to try to start you on a journey that could end in belief in God. I will come to 'God' in the final chapter. In a way, I wish I didn't have to announce the conclusion in advance. It would better to ask the question to which God might be the answer, rather than giving an answer to a question people may not have yet asked.

In exploring this, I want to start with the widest common ground, which is the feeling that there is something more than what we see around us. There seems to be a widespread sense of awe and wonder, though that can take many forms. When people are moved by natural beauty, or by great works of art, as they often are, there is often an instinctive feeling that there is something more. Wonder and reverence seem to be the gateway to sensing the spiritual world. Many people have the intuition that there is something more than the world that we see around us, call it God or not.

I want to start with experience and intuition rather than rational argument. I want to explore the grounds for the intuition that there is something more, but I am not looking for knock-down arguments one way or the other; they don't exist. Nevertheless, the sense that there is something more doesn't come from nowhere. It often starts with personal experience, but there are objective considerations from science that support those intuitions.

There is some interesting history here. The great medieval theologians produced what looked like rational proof of the existence of God, but they never imagined that they could be the starting point for a journey to faith. St Anselm, a great Archbishop of Canterbury of the eleventh century, developed some of these arguments, but he always understood their limitations. He assumed faith as the starting point and used these arguments to give it rational support. His motto was 'faith seeking understanding'. Faith comes first, understanding or rational argument comes later. In later centuries, some people tried to take these arguments out of the context of faith, hoping that they could stand alone, but I don't believe they can.

However, around 1800, there began to be a reaction against these rational arguments for the existence of God, notably with Friedrich Schleiermacher, often called the 'father of modern theology', and famous for his *On Religion: Speeches to its Cultured Despisers* (great title!). He wanted to get back to human feeling as the starting point for a journey to faith.

So, I will turn now to research on people's spiritual intuitions or experiences. You can do a survey of whether people have had what you might broadly call spiritual or religious experiences. The main UK survey is by David Hay, and the key question was 'Have you ever been aware of, or influenced by, a presence or power, whether you call it God or not, which is different from your everyday self?'

About a third of the population said 'yes' to that question. There are surveys with similar results in the USA. These experiences are often brief but powerful; they are memorable and life-changing. How people answer that question does not seem much related to conventional religious belief or to churchgoing. However, the people who answered 'yes' were those who thought that the 'spiritual side of life' was important.

Something of a division has grown up between those who are primarily religious and those that are primarily spiritual. The strong intuition that there is something more belongs to the 'spiritual' side of that divide. Whether or not people say that they have experienced something beyond themselves doesn't seem to depend much on culture or background. It is striking that the sense that there is something more is as common in the UK as in the USA, despite America being a much more religious country. It seems to be something that arises from the human constitution rather than from the culture around us.

Some people seem much more likely than others to have the intuition that there is something more. We don't yet fully understand what is involved in that, but it seems to depend in part on openness to experience. It seems that some people exercise much more control than others over their conscious experience; some people filter out more than others. The sense that there is something more may arise more strongly in people who filter out less of their potential experiences.

There also seems to be a strong intuitive spirituality in children, if you allow them to describe it in their own terms, and don't try to impose adult concepts on it. However, it often seems to fade as they move into their second decade of life. We don't quite know why that happens. It may be peer pressure, or it may be connected with the development of abstract adult thought.

> *Question:*
> *Do you have a feeling that there is something more?*
> *What in particular gives you that feeling?*

## More Than Matter

Let me now switch tack and bring in some rational arguments that support and shape the intuition that there is something more. I am going to lean on arguments that have a basis in science, rather than abstract philosophical arguments.

There is a widespread assumption among cosmologists like Stephen Hawking that there is something more than the world around us, something more than this world of space and time. Cosmologists assume some kind of Big Bang. The assumption is that space came into existence with the Big Bang, though it may have taken a few seconds for things to settle down to the three-dimensional space that we are all familiar with.

Cosmologists generally assume that time came into existence with the Big Bang, along with space. That is also what St Augustine thought a long time ago. He rejected the idea that there had always been time, and that at some point in time God created the world. He thought, rather, that God brought time into existence with Creation, i.e. that time was one of the things that God created.

This leads to the idea that our world of space and time somehow emerged from some other kind of reality that is over and above our space-time world or, as theologians would say, some transcendent reality. We are very unsure what that transcendent reality might be like. Our human thinking is so enmeshed with this space-time world that it is hard for us to think about any other. Theologians have found that too, of course.

One idea in scientific circles is that this non-spatio-temporal reality might be a 'quantum vacuum', i.e. the quantum state with the lowest possible energy. However, we don't need to concern ourselves with the details of that. The important point here is that cosmologists and religious people agree that there is some kind of transcendent reality, beyond this space-time world in which we live. Admittedly, they understand that non-space-time world very differently, but they agree that there is something more than space and time.

There is another similar point of agreement between religious people and physicists about what the world basically consists of, or at least about what it does *not* consist of. The common-sense idea is that it consists of bits of hard matter. But no physicist now thinks that the world consists of hard bits of material stuff. It may look and feel like that, but everyone now agrees that there is more going on underneath the surface. If materialism is the idea that the world basically consists of matter, no well-informed person is now a materialist. Materialism is finished. Religious people have long thought that there was more to the world than matter; now scientists agree.

So what do scientists think the world does consist of, if not matter? Probably energy. It has been said that the world is elegantly rearranged energy. Again, I'm not going to go into details. However, in broad-brush terms, atoms are not hard bits of matter. Inside atoms there are protons that have positive energy and electrons that have negative energy. It is all basically energy. There is a sense in which the two energies cancel each other out. In a nice phrase coined by the atheist scientist, Peter Atkins, the world is 'elegantly reorganised nothing'.

Atkins seems to think that this is an argument for atheism, but I don't see why. I marvel at how elegant the reorganisation of nothing is. It is also not a million miles from what theologians have been saying for centuries, that God created the universe out of nothing, though when you get down to details, it is not exactly the same. What theologians mean is that the creation of the world was not dependent on anything that existed previously; it was brought into existence from scratch.

Einstein had a famous equation that set out the relationship between matter and energy; they are two sides of the same coin. What seems to be energy can become matter, and vice versa. The intuition of scientists seems to be that energy is the more fundamental, and that matter is a translation or rearrangement of it.

Along similar lines there might be a physics of the future that says that the world is basically composed, not even of energy, but of 'information'. That is presently just a gleam in the eye of a few physicists, but the fact that it is proposed seriously at all shows how far we have come from the idea that the world consists of hard matter.

Religious people are not committed to the idea that the world is basically energy, or information either. They would probably say that reality is basically 'spiritual', and comes from a God who is spirit. However, physicists and religious thinkers agree that the world is not basically composed of matter, and that there is something beyond matter. Saying that the world is energy and saying that it is spirit are not the same, but the differences may be negotiable. In contrast, saying that the world is composed of matter would be on a more direct collision course with saying that it is basically spirit.

I said earlier that cosmologists and religious people don't agree about what there is beyond space and time, but they do now agree that there is something more. It is a parallel situation here. Physicists don't agree with religious people about exactly what there is beyond apparently hard matter, but they agree that there is something deeper than matter.

*Question:*

*Do you find that modern physics supports your sense that
there is something more?*

## Direction and Purpose

The last scientific pointer to something more than I want to consider
is about a sense of direction or purpose. It is often claimed that
science assumes that the world has no direction; that is a fundamental
difference from religion. But in fact there are now some points where
science is at least considering direction in the world.

Everyone agrees that the world we know is remarkably fine-tuned
to produce the conditions under which life can flourish. If the basic
laws of physics were even slightly different, the world would not
have produced life in the way it has. Everyone agrees about this basic
fact, but there is no agreement about why the world is fine-tuned in
the way it is. However, the fine-tuning invites the suggestion that
the world is as it is so as to be fruitful; there could be purpose and
direction behind it.

The fact is that the universe has been remarkably fruitful, but
it could very easily have been otherwise. The balance between the
force of expansion coming from the Big Bang and the force of gravity
pulling it back in again seems to be exactly right to give us a stable
planet on which life has a chance to develop.

Equally, conditions seem to be exactly right for the formation of
carbon, which is the basis of all life. Carbon is, on the face of it, an
element that is rather unlikely to form. It depends on three elements
of helium colliding. However, there is a nuclear resonance that is
exactly what is needed to help carbon to form. The atheist scientist,
Fred Hoyle, once commentated that it looks as though someone has
been monkeying with the physics.

Everything seems exactly right to make the universe stable, fruitful
and beautiful. I am not trying to say that proves that there is a God,
but the universe fits with what God would presumably have wanted,
i.e. it is orderly and fruitful. It is one of a number of things that is
consistent with belief in God and points in that direction.

The evolution of life also seems to have direction. If you look at the
evidence from the fossil record of how life has changed, the changes
are not random; there is clearly direction behind the changes.

Roughly speaking, the direction is towards more complex forms of life. Actually I think the key change may be towards forms of life that have increasingly good awareness of the world around them. That in turn may have led to a species like us humans that has thought and language, and which is able to become aware of spiritual realities.

Showing that there is direction in evolution isn't the same as showing that there is purpose. I think the evidence for direction is overwhelming and cannot really be denied. However, you can only really talk about purpose if you assume that there is a Being with intentions. That is further than science can go, but neither does science rule purpose out. Science can show that there is direction in evolution. However, interpreting that in terms of purpose brings in a different kind of perspective, one that goes beyond what science can establish. It is a point at which religious people can legitimately offer an interpretation of the direction in a world for which science has provided evidence.

> *Question:*
>
> *Do you have a sense that there is direction*
> *and purpose in life?*
>
> *What gives you that sense?*

## Souls and Angels

There are also strong intuitions about the afterlife and about spiritual beings. Though belief in God has been declining in the post-war period, belief in the afterlife has actually been increasing, both in Europe and America. There is considerably more belief in an afterlife in America than in Europe; but, in both cases, belief in life beyond death has been increasing.

Belief in an afterlife can take different forms. Some such belief is specifically based in religion. However, there is also a mystical or experiential approach to immortality that is not dependent on religious faith, in which people feel that the distinction between life and death is transcended. It may be that in some cases, belief in immortality starts from the conviction that one's own death will not be the end, whereas in other cases the focus is more on continuing contact with those who have died.

In some cases, belief in the afterlife arises from seeing the human being as composed of body and soul, with the soul able to continue after death when the body dies. In other cases, belief in an afterlife is grounded less in the human constitution and more in an eternal God, through whom immortality is possible for humans.

Religious faiths have different traditions. Belief in the afterlife is stronger in Christianity than Judaism and stronger among Catholics than Protestants. We don't yet know much about belief in the afterlife among those who are more spiritual than religious, and what form that takes. However, it seems likely that forms of belief in the afterlife that are specifically grounded in religious faith are in decline, and that it is other forms of belief in the afterlife that are increasing.

There is much recent interest in trying to find support for an afterlife, both through scientific research on near-death experiences and reincarnation, and from practices such as spiritualist mediumship. It is striking how differently the evidence on near-death experiences has been interpreted. Some are convinced by reductionist explanations in terms of brain malfunction; others think there is compelling evidence for an afterlife. At present it seems that everyone brings their presuppositions to how to interpret the evidence and very few people change their mind as a result of it.

Among those who believe in an afterlife, there are significant differences over how to relate to the departed. I am inclined to think that, though some quiet sense of connection with the departed can be helpful, it is not appropriate to try to involve them in human affairs in too specific a way, as spiritualism tried to do. Neither is it helpful for the departed to stay around after physical death in the form of ghosts or hauntings. Some requests for exorcism probably related to spirits of the departed who need to go to their rest, rather than to evil spirits; that calls for a different approach.

I suspect that belief in guardian angels has been increasing too, though there is less good research data on that. It seems that a significant proportion of people now talk about angels coming to support them in times of danger, many of whom are not churchgoers.

Angels are more mysterious than the departed. They are, for example, beings of light who can move instantly from one place to another. However, as Rupert Sheldrake and Matthew Fox have pointed out, there seems to be an uncanny similarity between what classic theologians say about angels, and what modern physics says about photons. The world of angels may seem to defy common sense, but some modern physics also defies common sense in similar ways.

Belief in departed souls and in angels may well now be running more strongly among those who do not go to church than among those who do. People are clearly not giving up on the idea that there is 'something more', some kind of spiritual world, but there seems to be a movement towards recognising spirits of the departed and angels, and away from belief in God. It seems that the spiritual world is being reconceptualised rather than dismissed.

> *Question:*
> *Are angels and departed souls a reality that you know*
> *from experience?*

## Spiritual and/or Religious

Even among those who are open to recognising a spiritual world that is beyond the world of matter and the everyday world, there are now multiple ways of conceptualising it, and complex relationships between them. There are those who are religious in one of the traditional ways; in contrast, there are those who see themselves as 'spiritual but not religious'.

Often there is a mutual suspicion and antagonism between these two groups. However, there are also many people with sympathies in both camps. At this point I probably need to declare my own position. My personal background is with Christianity, which is where my primary loyalties lie. However, I also have connections and sympathies with those who would say they are more spiritual than religious.

I share some of the criticisms of mainline churches made by those who are more spiritual than religious. Like them, I think the Church is often self-important and self-preoccupied. It often does not seem faithful to Jesus, and indeed seems less interested in Jesus than in its own survival. It seems to value church attendance more highly than the spiritual life and personal transformation. It often talks about God in a way that is simplistic and too anthropomorphic (something that I will return to in the final chapter). These failings alienate many people from the Church who would actually like to connect with it.

However, these are failings of contemporary churches; they are not problems with Jesus, or with Christian spirituality, practice and faith. Sadly, the mainline churches seem to have little understanding of how and why they are alienating people, and so do not understand what they need to do about it. The hope of many church people seems to be that it will suffice to adopt a more managerialist approach, or to dumb things down (as in 'messy church'). That seems to be a failure to grasp the nature of the problem.

The key question, as I see it, about the spirituality of those who are 'more spiritual than religious' is whether or not their spirituality sets forward the purposes of God. I believe it often does and that it probably reflects the work of the Holy Spirit. Connecting with the spirituality movement that is growing up outside the churches creates the opportunity of developing a way of living that is deeply rooted in the values and perspective of Jesus and in spiritual practice.

There may be a parallel with Jesus' attitude to his own Jewish people and to the gentile world beyond. Jesus was a Jew and started from the assumption that the Jews were God's chosen people. However, there is much in Jesus' life and teaching that suggests that he often despaired of their ability to understand what he was about and was trying to accomplish. That seems to have led him to reach out to Samaritans and Gentiles in the hope that they would get the point better. The Jews may have been God's chosen people, but many seemed to miss the opportunity and invitation that Jesus extended to them.

There is a parallel between church people now and the Jews of Jesus' time. The Church is the 'household of faith', and you would expect and hope that church people would be the first to understand what Jesus was about. However, church people often seem to get the point no better than the Jews of Jesus' time. Jesus' response was to reach out beyond his own chosen people. I suspect that, in our own time, God is reaching out beyond the churches, because church people who profess to be loyal to him have become distracted by other preoccupations. As a Christian, I am excited by the growing belief that there is something more, and by the growing commitment to spiritual practices such as mindfulness.

*Question:*

*What, for you, is the difference between religion and spirituality?*

## Bible Study

In some parts of the Old Testament there is a strong tendency to see God at work in nature, for example in Psalm 18:7–15. However, in the Old Testament, there is a gradual transition to sensing the presence of God in silence. A key passage is Elijah's experience of God in a 'sound of sheer silence' (1 Kings 19:11–13).

Angels play an important role in the Bible; it may be interesting to look again at the story of the birth of Jesus in Matthew's Gospel (Matthew 1:8–2:23) and notice the role played by angels there. Jesus, in his time in the wilderness (Matthew 4:1–11), encountered the devil and, at the end, angels. Notice how all this is presented in a matter-of-fact way.

Jesus does not have much to say about what we would now regard as religious belief, but he clearly had a close relationship with his unseen 'heavenly Father'. In John's Gospel, in particular, there are frequent references to the Father in almost every chapter. One Father to the Father is given in full, before Jesus' arrest (John 17).

St Paul has a strong sense that the living and the departed are one in Christ, for example in Romans 14:7–9.

## Background and Sources

There is helpful background in Fraser Watts (2017) *Psychology, Religion and Spirituality*. Cambridge University Press (especially chapter eight on spirituality).

David Hay has written several useful books. For his survey data see David Hay (1982) *Exploring Inner Space: Scientists and Religious Experience*. Penguin.

On children's spirituality, see David Hay and Rebecca Nye (2006) *The Spirit of the Child*. Jessica Kingsley. On more general issues, see David Hay (2006) *Something There: The Biology of the Human Spirit*. Darton, Longman & Todd.

On evidence from physics, see David A. Wilkinson (1993) *God, the Big Bang and Stephen Hawking*. Monarch Books. Or Keith Ward (2008) *The Big Questions in Science and Religion*. Templeton Press. On evolution see Simon Conway Morris (2015) *The Runes of Evolution: How the Universe Became Self-Aware*. Templeton Press. For an atheist perspective see Peter Atkins (1993) *Creation Revisited: The Origin of Space, Time and the Universe*. W.H. Freeman.

On life beyond death, see Paul Badham (2013) *Making Sense of Death and Immortality.* SPCK. For more detail on changing patterns of life in life beyond death see Ralph W. Hood, Peter C. Hill and Bernard Spilka (2009) *The Psychology of Religion: An Empirical Approach.* 4th Edition. Guilford Press. Chapter seven. On angels see Matthew Fox and Rupert Sheldrake (2014) *The Physics of Angels: Exploring the Realm Where Science and Spirit Meet.* Monkfish Book Publishing.

# Chapter Ten
## *Darkness and Light*

One of the key issues we all face on our personal and spiritual journey is that of good and evil. Light and dark seem very intertwined. It seems we can't go far into the light without having to engage with dark as well. In this chapter I will explore various aspects of how darkness and light are intertwined in our journey, how they are intertwined in ourselves, in events around us, and even in God.

## Mixed Experiences of Ourselves

Many people have mixed feelings about themselves. Some people have a very dark view of themselves, especially when they are depressed. Other people think highly of themselves and can't see anything wrong. Yet others see both good and bad in themselves. Sometimes it is hard to see the connection between the two, hard to understand how we (or others) could do both good and bad things.

There is often a gap between intentions and actions, with our intentions being better than our actions. Most of us at least mean well most of the time, but the follow-through on our good intentions can be disappointingly sporadic, both to ourselves and others. I recognise this in myself, so this is a heartfelt chapter. If you recognise this in yourself too, and feel a bit demoralised about it, you are in good company. St Paul, in one of the more heartfelt personal passages in his epistles, laments how he does things that he meant not to do, and fails to do the things he intended (Romans 7:14–25).

Qualities that work well for us in some situations can cause us trouble in others. Personal relationships and working life often call for different qualities, so people often find they do better at one than the other. Being cool and driven can help someone to be successful at work, but the same qualities may make it hard for them to build close and warm relationships.

Similarly, the same emotions can be good or bad. Guilt can be a helpful corrective when we are going off the rails, but it can also drag us down and become incapacitating. Anger can energise us in a good cause, but it can also be very destructive.

Many great people turn out to have 'feet of clay'. They can have remarkable achievements in some areas that are valued very highly, but behave incredibly badly in others. In fact, this seems to be very common, not just something found in a few 'bad apples'.

It is one of the greatest challenges of personal development to recognise our very mixed qualities, and to work at understanding how that arises. We may then be able to take steps to integrate things better. If that goes well, we will reach a point where we are less surprised by how we mess up sometimes, and actually let ourselves down less often.

The psychologist C.G. Jung used the word 'shadow' to refer to the dark side of the personality that can let us down badly, when so much else may seem admirable and impressive. It is a key question for many of us how to manage our shadow side, so it doesn't destroy or sabotage what is good in our personality.

His basic advice is to bring our shadow in from the cold and to integrate it better with the rest of us. As I said before when reflecting on the theme of wholeness, the alternatives of ignoring it, or trying to eradicate it, don't seem to work. Condemning our shadow doesn't seem to work; it is better to befriend it and harness it for good.

Other psychologists have used different terminology for the problem of recognising both good and bad in ourselves. Freudians think about somewhat related issues in terms of 'splitting', the tendency to think of things as all good or all bad, and to struggle to recognise the complex way in which the two jostle together. Cognitive psychologists talk about 'cognitive complexity' or 'integrative complexity', contrasting it with more black-and-white thinking. Integrative thinkers try to hold everything together, and to see both the good and the bad.

We are none of us all good or all bad. The path of personal development lies in recognising that, and in coming to terms with it.

*Question:*

*Do you feel you are mainly good, mainly bad, or a puzzling mixture of the two?*

## Different Perspectives

There are always different viewpoints and perspectives of ourselves. We have our own point of view of ourselves. We may actually have more than one view of ourselves, depending on what situation we are in, or our mood at the time. There are also the viewpoints of others, and inevitably some people will think better of us than others.

This can all be quite bewildering. What looks good from one point of view can look very different from another vantage point. It is humbling to realise that we never get the complete picture. For those who have a sense of the presence of God, it can be helpful to try to enter into a God's eye perspective of ourselves. I assume that will be more balanced and complete than what we can manage, left to ourselves.

We tend to divide experiences up into positive and negative experiences, things we like and things we don't like. But that is a very limited perspective and, on a spiritual journey through life, I think we are increasingly challenged to see things differently. Ignatius of Loyola, who founded the Jesuits, suggested that the more important distinction is between things that bring us closer to God and things that separate us further from him. He called them 'consolations' and 'desolations'. For Christians that is a more important distinction.

There is not much connection between these two distinctions. You can have pleasant experiences that leave us further away from God, and many indulgences are like that. You can also have unpleasant experiences that are helpful in a challenging way and can bring us closer to God.

The human perspective itself on the natural world is rather limited. We see and hear sounds within certain frequencies but, for example, there are some sounds that are too high for us to hear, though bats can hear them. Our perspective of ourselves is even more limited. We never see the whole picture. God has the bigger picture and the hope is that, as our spiritual life develops, we will see more of that bigger picture.

We also have to take into account that our perspective is not just limited, but actually a bit distorted. Imagine light shining through a prism. The light starts white, pure white light, but after going through a prism it becomes all the colours of the rainbow. Think of the white light as being the pure light that shines from God. We are like prisms. After the light has gone through us, with all our distortions, insecurities, lusts and all the rest, it no longer looks to be the pure light it was at source.

The spiritual journey involves gradually being liberated from our partial and distorted perspectives. We need that liberation in many areas of our life, but we need it most when it comes to understanding ourselves better. Jesus told his disciples that 'when the Spirit of truth comes, he will guide you into all truth' (John 16:13). It is often about ourselves that we most urgently need that full truth.

> *Question:*
>
> *Do you find it hard to know the 'truth' about yourself?*
> *Are there aspects of yourself where it is especially hard*
> *to recognise the truth?*

## Problematic Events

Just as there is a dark side to each individual, there is often a dark side to events in the public world, and again good and evil are so intertwined that we can't quite be sure what we are dealing with.

It often seems impossible to have good without evil. They are often two sides of the same coin, and you can't have a coin with just one side. The same scientific advances that can improve the quality of human life can also be enormously destructive when used in warfare. Many events in the natural world, such as volcanoes, have a range of consequences, some good, some harmful. The harmful consequences are often more immediate, but there are also long-term benefits in terms of the fertility of land etc.

Context is important. Evolutionary developments that may have very negative consequences in one situation can be life-saving in another. Different challenges call for different solutions; what is harmful, or evil, depends on context. In these various ways, I think it is plausible to argue that good and evil are often inextricably intertwined.

Human achievements often turn out to have a sting in the tail that undermines what had seemed to be a real advance. Society often seems naïve about this. Just as individuals can have blind spots about their failings, so society often seems surprised that what, from one point of view, seems to be progress can also have very damaging consequences.

As a society we have many urgent problems to sort out, and it is becoming clear that, unless we change how we do things, we are heading for serious crises on multiple fronts. In many areas of life, recent events have warned us of the dangers we are in. Some people might see this as a challenge from God to sort ourselves out and do things differently.

Take the banking crisis and all that has followed from it. We had learned to manage our economic life in ways that considerably increased our prosperity. However, at the same time, we had collectively slipped into a very greedy culture that placed too much weight on seeking extreme wealth, regardless of the consequences. We can see the resulting crisis as some kind of judgement from God, starkly facing us with the consequences of our actions.

There are similar issues about global warming, which is the flip side of developments that have enhanced human flourishing and improved the quality of life. We are now facing serious problems that flow from our inconsiderate and irresponsible use of the planet and its resources. That can also be seen as reflecting the judgement of God.

The same is true of the consequences of a nuclear holocaust which arises from human hatred and intolerance, and which at any moment could make the planet uninhabitable. That can also be seen as a judgement of God for misusing scientific advances.

All these various problems I see as essentially moral and spiritual problems. Humanity seems sadly lacking in moral and spiritual maturity, with the result that we are close to destroying ourselves. We face a stark choice of either growing up in moral and spiritual terms, or destroying ourselves. The judgement of God is facing us with that stark choice.

*Question:*

*Do you feel that there is a 'message' of some kind to humanity
in the many challenges we face?*

## The Anger and Judgement of God

It may seem strange and old-fashioned to talk about the judgement of
God. You may ask how that relates to the goodness of God. I suggest
that we are sometimes too simplistic about what we mean by the
'goodness' of God, and I want to look again at that. Some experiences
can seem so negative that they challenge our belief in the goodness
of God, but they need not do so.

There is much in the Bible, and in Christian thinking, about the
anger and judgement of God. If you feel yourself to be on the receiving
end of that, you may indeed feel yourself to be in touch with the dark
side of God. Then you may well wonder how that relates to what one
of the Epistles of John says about God being light, and that in him
there is no darkness at all (1 John 1:5).

We may also think that talk of the anger and judgement of God is
an Old Testament view of God, and not part of the God of love we
see in Jesus. But that would be wrong. Jesus gets angry, and that helps
us to understand the nature of God's anger. All the Gospels describe
occasions when Jesus appears, from what he says and does, to be
angry. He is evidently angry when he goes into the temple courtyard
and overturns the tables of the money-changers who were converting
ordinary currency into temple currency at extortionate rates.

One of the Gospels, Mark, explicitly says that Jesus got angry,
or indignant. There are two occasions. One is when people are
complaining about him healing people on the Sabbath (Mark 3:1–6);
the other is when people are trying to keep children away from him
(Mark 10:13–14). In both cases, Mark explicitly says that Jesus was
angry or indignant. Interestingly, Matthew and Luke tell the same
stories, probably drawing on Mark which was written earlier, but they
drop the explicit statement that Jesus was angry; but I am pleased we
have it at least in Mark.

Does Jesus' anger mean that he is not 'good' after all? I don't think
so. His anger is part of his goodness. In the same way, I take God's
anger to be part of his goodness. The key issue lies in exactly what

makes people angry. There is sometimes called 'righteous' anger. Jesus was made angry by unnecessary obstacles to God's free outpouring of love, and by the hypocrisy that made a travesty of religion, subverting it so that it obstructed God's purposes rather than setting them forward. That kind of anger is an aspect of goodness. Our own anger (mine at least) often reveals just how small-minded we are.

The Bible also talks about 'judgement', and that can also sound unpalatable to modern ears. Certainly, judgementalism is bad; no one should be the victim of arbitrary and hostile judgements. But there is also judgement that is fair and just, and that can be helpful. There is also having good judgement ourselves, especially good judgement about ourselves. I hope we would all want that. Judgement is not always something to fear, though it can be challenging.

So, when Jesus talks about coming into the world to bring judgement, as he does, (John 9:39), I think he is essentially talking about coming into the world to bring good judgement. That is a gift, and ultimately a very welcome one, even though the transition from a biased self-serving perspective to good judgement can be challenging and initially unwelcome.

The main Greek word for judgement in the Gospels, especially John, is 'krisis', from which we get our word 'crisis'. It is a crossroads, a choice point, the point where fudging issues, and trying to pretend that black is white, has to stop. That is undoubtedly challenging, but ultimately very much in our best interests.

*Question:*
*What sense can you make of the 'anger'*
*and judgement of God?*

## Is God 'Good'?

I think we can make some headway with these difficult questions by getting more subtle, less black and white, in our thinking. I suggest that there may be a side of God that we humans experience as being dark, but which comes from love and from which we benefit. God is perhaps not always as nice and pleasant as we might like, any more than Jesus is always 'gentle Jesus, meek and mild', as the hymn claims.

We might think about parenting and apply that, by analogy, to God. As we have seen, if children are going to grow up well, they need a combination of two different things. They need to feel loved, cared for and understood. But they also need some clear guidance, some setting of boundaries, and some expectations which they can try to meet.

If we experience God as not always being nice to us, that doesn't necessarily mean that he is not being good to us. 'Niceness' is about what we like; 'goodness', I suggest, takes a broader view of what is helpful to us. We certainly need the nurture of God, but we may also need his judgement. It can be perfectly compatible with a sense of the love and goodness of God to sometimes feel that we are being judged by God. However, that does involve a broader way of thinking about goodness.

My point is that the idea that God is dark and threatening arises in part from failing to realise that God, like a good parent, has to be challenging in order to act in our best interests. If God doesn't look good to us, that may in part be because of our limited perception.

From the late nineteenth century onwards, there has been a remarkable shift in how people have seen God. People used to talk about the punishment of God in a way that induced fear. But we have increasingly moved away from that. We may have ended up with a God who is too nice.

Interestingly, one of the people who protested most loudly about this in the twentieth century was C.G. Jung. He was very aware of the important role played by what he called the 'shadow' in a whole person, and emphatic that the path to personal wholeness involved healing and integrating the shadow side of our personality, not trying to pretend it wasn't there or trying to just jettison it. He saw people who were trying to pretend that there was no shadow side to God as like people trying to pretend they themselves had no shadow.

I have talked about the 'anger' and 'judgement' of God, but I am not actually completely happy with that way of language. When we talk about the anger or judgement of God we are not assuming that God is behaving like a cross human being and deciding to punish us. We are saying that this deepest reality of all, whom we call 'God', sometimes faces us rather starkly with the consequences of our stupid actions. That is what I mean by his 'judgement', and it can be a source of blessing to us.

I would rather talk about the 'challenge' of God, a challenge that faces us in rather unpalatable ways with the consequences of our actions and challenges us to change. If we are to talk about the 'judgement' of God, we need to rescue that word from some of its usual connotations. I think God always speaks words to us of promise and hope; there is always a forward-looking purpose, even when God may be facing us with the consequences of our past actions.

*Question:*

*What does it mean to say that
God is 'good'?*

## God as All

Words for God are linked to one of two roots. In some languages like English, the word for God is linked to 'good'. In other languages, including Aramaic, the language that Jesus spoke, the word for God is linked to 'all'. There is bound to be a tension here. Not everything is good, so how can God be 'good', and also be 'all'?

Christians may have different instincts when faced with this puzzle. We seem on the horns of a dilemma. If you say that some things don't come from God and have an independent origin, that sets up a rival source of things, a kind of alternative anti-God who is the source of suffering and evil. If you say that everything comes from God, you are implying that suffering and evil come from God.

There are thus basically two different approaches. One is that there are two separate and unconnected forces in the world, one good and the other evil, and that the force for good happens to be stronger. The other approach, and the one that mainline Christianity has always adopted, is to say that there is only one fundamental cosmic force (that people call 'God'), which is fundamentally good. In as far as there is evil in the world, it must arise in some way from that basic force of goodness; it cannot have a separate, independent origin.

That is a more integrationist position, and it seems to be the preferable alternative, however difficult it may be to explain how basic goodness could somehow give rise to evil. One way of explaining that is to say that evil is insubstantial, that it is really just an absence of goodness. However, if pressed too far, that is unconvincing, given the ever-present reality of evil around us.

Another attempted solution is to postulate an historical event that led the original goodness of Creation to become 'fallen'. I have no problem in saying that Creation is fallen; in one sense that is just obviously correct at a descriptive level. However, I think there are insuperable problems in trying to postulate an historical event that led to Creation becoming fallen. I see no prospect of being able to overcome the problems that dog the concept of a historical fall. It is, in any case, a post-Biblical idea. Genesis 3 is often pressed into service as the story of the fall, but that is to read more into the text than is actually there.

I don't have a neat solution to these problems. However, my instinct is to hang on to the belief that God is all, and that everything has its origin in him and holds together in him. St Paul is very emphatic that all things in Heaven and earth were created through and for Christ (Colossians 1:16). However, as I have said, I think there is scope for rethinking what we mean by the 'goodness' of God, and that goes some way to softening the problem.

Which way one goes on these issues may have much bigger practical consequences than are at first apparent. A view of God that goes too far towards excluding anything dark from the image of God can also lead to an idealisation of religion. That can be quite dangerous, as it is when religion is idealised that people become fanatical about it, and think that it provides a rationale for evil and destructive behaviour.

So, I think it is always healthier to integrate light and darkness rather than to separate them. However, I would want to hang on to the widespread spiritual intuition (one that Christians share with others), that ultimately, despite current appearances, the forces of light and goodness are stronger. We feel instinctively that truth gets closer to the heart of things than lies, that beauty gets closer to the heart of things than ugliness, and that goodness gets closer to the heart of things than evil. Among affirmations to have come out of Christianity, I think the one that would command widespread assent is one from Desmond Tutu: 'Goodness is stronger than evil; love is stronger than hate; light is stronger than darkness; life is stronger than death.'

*Question:*
*Do you agree that goodness is stronger than evil?*
*If so, what makes you think that?*

# The Dark Night

Finally in this chapter, I want to look at the dark and difficult aspects of the spiritual journey, and at how darkness and light are intertwined there.

Once the heart starts to connect with God, it wants to go on connecting. But then come the times when we long for that connection, but find that it doesn't quite happen. There are times when we feel that God is distant; he seems to be absent when we need him. God may appear with remarkable power and directness when we don't expect him. Many people have described their experience of trying to pray in a regular, disciplined way, but felt that they were not really connecting with anything. That is what St John of the Cross called the *Dark Night of the Soul*. What is going on there?

Firstly, this feeling that God is absent may actually be a false and distorted perception of ours. Many people can testify that what initially felt like the absence of God proved, with hindsight, to have been a necessary transition to a different kind of relationship with God, in which God was less 'in our faces', but still very much present in a more internalised and constant way. It can be a transition from a childlike attachment relationship to God being our constant but hidden companion. But we can often only recognise that transition with hindsight.

Secondly, a distinction is often made between the *feeling* of connection with God and God himself. The heart's sense of connection with God may get closer than the head trying to get to know *about* God by thinking about him. But perhaps it is still not quite the real thing. I said in the first chapter that the heart's relationship to God is the real thing, but maybe I should correct that. The way of the heart may be closer, but still not quite the real thing. Perhaps we need not only to move beyond thinking about God, but also to go beyond the God we relate to with feeling.

In fact, the dark night of the soul may ultimately be good for us because it helps to liberate us from our attachments. It is fundamentally about liberation. As I said earlier, what we like and what is in our best interests are different things. The dark night may actually help to liberate us from being over-attached to what we like, even if we don't always like that liberation.

This 'dark night' may only be dark in the sense of being 'obscure'; it is a darkness in which we can't easily see our way, but it is not dark in the sense of being 'sinister'. People who have followed this path often say that the darkness is necessary for our protection; if we could see more clearly we would take fright.

Finally, the path through the darkness is one on which we need to be led. We don't have it within us to take ourselves on this path. We have to let the something beyond take over; it is like people allowing themselves to play the natural game of tennis, rather than trying to plot their moves. I will return to that analogy shortly.

> *Question:*
>
> *Does your spiritual life sometimes lead you through a 'dark' time?*

## Bible Study

For St Paul's lament about how his intentions and actions don't match up, see Romans 7:14–25.

The word 'judgement' has different connotations in Matthew and John, the two Gospels that it is used in most. Matthew often assumes that 'judgement' means condemnation, as in Matthew 5:21–22. The story of the sheep and the goats, Matthew 25:31–46, is also in effect a story about judgement, and separating one group from another, even though it doesn't use the word. John uses 'judgement' more as seeing things clearly, as in John 3:19–21 and 7:24.

Jesus is a good role model for when and how to be angry. Mark is the Gospel that is most explicit about the anger and indignation of Jesus. See Mark 3:1–6 over healing on the Sabbath, and Mark 10:13–16 over keeping children from him. Anger is also implicit in the cleansing of the temple in Mark 11:15–19. You might like to compare Jesus' anger with your own.

St Paul has a strong sense of there being both good and evil in the spiritual world. Mostly he is very positive about what is spiritual but note that he is also aware of spiritual evil, see Ephesians 6:12.

## Background and Sources

An interesting study of the personal failings of many highly esteemed gurus is Anthony Storr (1997) *Feet of Clay: Study of Gurus.* HarperCollins. For a general psychological approach to how we can do puzzlingly inconsistent things, see Joseph Burgo (2012) *Why Do I Do That? Psychological Defense Mechanisms and the Hidden Ways They Shape Our Lives*. New Rise Press.

I have discussed a Christian view of anger in Fraser Watts (2007) 'Emotion Regulation and Religion', in James J. Gross (ed.) *Handbook of Emotion Regulation*. New York: Guilford Press. pp. 504–20.

Jung took a strong position on the reality of evil, which is examined in Howard Littleton Philp (1959) *Jung and the Problem of Evil*. R. M. McBride. The darkness of God is discussed from the dual perspectives of Jungian ideas about the shadow and a concern about nuclear weapons in Jim Garrison (1982) *The Darkness of God: Theology After Hiroshima*. SCM Press. See also Matthias Beier (2004) *A Violent God-Image: An Introduction to the Work of Eugen Drewermann*. Continuum.

An excellent psychological study of how the idealisation of religion can bring out the best and worst in humanity is James W. Jones (2002) *Terror and Transformation: The Ambiguity of Religion in Psychoanalytic Perspective*. Routledge. For a general psychological account of how evil arises see Roy F. Baumeister (1999) *Evil: Inside Human Violence and Cruelty*. Henry Holt and Company. For a philosophical perspective see Mary Midgley (2001) *Wickedness: A Philosophical Essay*. Routledge.

A good psychologically oriented book on the dark night of the soul is Gerald G. May (2004) *The Dark Night of the Soul: A Psychiatrist Explores the Connection Between Darkness and Spiritual Growth*. HarperSanFrancisco.

# Chapter Eleven
## *Jesus*

In this chapter I want to turn to thinking about Jesus. Attitudes to Jesus are generally quite positive. Jesus is widely admired, and debates about him have not generally been about that, but about whether or not he was God.

What we know about Jesus comes largely from the Gospels. However, they were written by his followers, and some time after his crucifixion. Even Mark, the first of them, was written at least thirty years after Jesus' death. Are they historically reliable? In broad terms, I think they are, if not in every detail. There is no doubt that Jesus lived and was crucified; he is not a fictional creation.

Mark's Gospel seems to be in two parts, and may have been compiled from different sources. The first half is about Jesus' life, and the second about his arrest, trial and death. Mark has nothing about Jesus' birth and early life, and begins the story with Jesus being baptised by John. It probably also said nothing originally about his Resurrection, though there is some dispute about that among scholars. The claims about Jesus in the Christian Creeds have little connection with what Mark's Gospel says about him, except that he was 'crucified, dead and buried'. I will return to claims about Jesus and will start from what we know from the Gospels about Jesus himself.

## Jesus as Healer

Mark presents Jesus primarily as a healer and miracle worker. It might be thought that that was just unreliable exaggeration on the part of Jesus' followers. However, the indications are that Jesus was accepted by independent observers like Josephus as a 'doer of startling deeds'. This is not to say that every detail of the healing stories in the Gospels is necessarily correct, but it seems highly likely that the general picture that emerges of Jesus as a healer is authentic.

Jesus lived in a culture where such healing was not unknown, and he was probably one of a number of miracle workers operating in Palestine at the time, though apparently a notable one. In saying that Jesus was a healer, I am not necessarily claiming that he was unique. He probably did not regard himself as unique as a healer and, according to the Gospels, expected his disciples to be healers too.

I am also not necessarily saying that Jesus' healings were completely supernatural. In general, I don't want to separate natural and supernatural elements too sharply. Where there are healings of the body there are obviously natural biological processes involved. There will also be psychological processes involved, about hope and trust, for example. I don't want to say that the healings of Jesus, or spiritual healings now, are nothing but the result of ordinary physical and psychological processes; but I do think they work through those processes.

So what is extra in 'faith' healing or 'spiritual' healing? There is strong evidence that engaging in spiritual practices such as prayer or meditation is associated with good health, so it is not surprising that when a healer and the person who needs healing pray together, there are similar health benefits.

There are also probably relational elements. Something can catch fire when two people come together to pray for healing that is more than the sum of both people praying separately. This would have been particularly true of Jesus who clearly had enormous spiritual charisma. I suspect that healing is most powerful when there is a strong 'chemistry' between the healer and the person being healed.

That 'catching fire' can take on an extra dimension when both the healer and person being healed connect with spiritual resources beyond themselves, whether they think of those resources in terms of a personal God or in some other way. Jesus seems to have been especially good (some would say uniquely good) at doing that.

People flocked around Jesus largely because of his healings, in a way that he sometimes found overwhelming, and needed to escape from. However, he does not seem to have minded meeting people's needs, nor minded people seeking him out because they had needs he could meet. Church people sometimes don't like people 'using' religion just for what is in it for them, but Jesus does not seem to have minded.

*Question:*

*Would you agree that Jesus was a remarkable healer?*

*If so, what significance does that have for you?*

## Encounters with Jesus

Jesus' words as recorded in the Gospels fall into two main groups: there are conversations with individual discourses, and more general discourses delivered to groups, which consist mainly of stories. From this I think we can glean something of what Jesus is trying to achieve. Jesus has often been held up as a great moral teacher, if not the Son of God. However, I think it misrepresents Jesus to call him a 'great moral teacher'. He is not really an educator, and he is certainly not moralistic.

What he says to people often seems very specific to them and to the situation; he doesn't seem to be trying to set out timeless moral truths, but rather to respond to each situation in which he finds himself. You can infer something of his general approach from the specific examples, but it is not Jesus' style to try to speak general moral truths that will apply to all people for all time. He is very contextual in his approach.

He also seems quite practical and immediate and wants people to actually live differently. The way he challenges the various fishermen to join him at the outset is characteristic. He is disturbing and unsettling. He is himself a vagrant leading what was necessarily an unpredictable life, and he draws other people out of their settled routine into his own unsettled and unsettling approach to life. Rather than trying to tell people how to live, he is encouraging them to join him in how he is living.

He tells stories and uses images and analogies. The usual comment on that is that people pay better attention to stories, and it shows what a good teacher Jesus is that he uses stories. But sometimes people were clearly puzzled by Jesus' stories and were left wondering what they meant. According to the Gospels, Jesus says that he deliberately left people puzzled (Matthew 13:10–15). It seems that Jesus may have wanted to keep people puzzling, rather than imagining that they understood him.

Looking at the various people Jesus meets and how he interacts with them, I suggest that you can discern some common strands. He often encourages people to believe that things can be better, to look for a 'pearl of great value' (Matthew 13:45–46). When he meets Nicodemus, he reminds him of Jacob's vision of a ladder between Heaven and earth and angels going up and down. He doesn't want people to settle for second best; he encourages people to go for the very best.

Next, he points out how challenging that will be and what sacrifices will have to be made. People will have to give up what they already have if they are to find what is really worthwhile. Jesus is very forthright about how half-heartedness will get us nowhere; his approach is 'all or nothing'.

The third strand is one of reassurance, that if you get your priorities right and make the necessary sacrifices, things will actually work out; you will find the wind is behind you, and that your 'heavenly Father' will take care of you. In the end, Jesus reassures people, all the sacrifices will be worthwhile; it will be challenging but you won't be on your own.

*Question:*

*What do you see as the essence of Jesus' teaching?*

## Jesus and Recovery of the Lost

I want now to turn from the story of Jesus to the stories that Jesus told. Jesus tells several stories about recovery of the lost. I am going to take these as applying to the lost or wayward aspects of our personalities, and explore their implications.

I am not necessarily saying that Jesus had this application of his stories specifically in mind when he told them. However, it is part of the genius of Jesus' stories that they have a rich range of applications, some of which may only unfold in different circumstances from those in which the stories were told.

Chapter fifteen of Luke's Gospel is devoted entirely to stories about recovery of the lost:

- the lost sheep, which strays off over the mountains and is searched for and brought back to join the other ninety-nine in the fold;
- the lost coin that the woman searches for until it is back with the other nine;
- the lost (or 'prodigal') son who goes off to lead a dissolute life, but returns to his father and is welcomed back with much rejoicing.

When applied to human personality, the implication is that the lost or wayward parts of our personalities are to be searched for and brought back into the fold to join the more obviously acceptable parts of our personalities, and there is to be much rejoicing over the recovery of these lost aspects of our selves, more than over other parts where no recovery is needed.

When Jung talks about the importance of the 'shadow' part of our personalities, and about the importance of integrating it so that we become whole, he is just expressing in modern terminology what is implicit in Jesus' stories when they are applied to human personality. It is recovery of the lost that makes us 'whole'. As we saw in chapter five, there is a close connection between healing and wholeness, and the two words come from the same root. In fact, being 'healed' and becoming 'whole' mean much the same thing.

There is a parallel application to human society, implying that society is healed when 'lost' members of society, who have dropped out of it in some way, are 'found' and brought back into the fold of society, which is thereby made whole.

Alongside this strand of radical inclusiveness in Jesus' stories about recovery of the lost, there is another strand that needs to be considered. That is about the importance of having clear priorities, and being willing to sacrifice less important things to go for what is really important. It is seen, for example, in Jesus' story about selling everything else to buy one pearl of great value. It is one of a series of such stories found in Matthew 13:36–52. At first sight, this seems to sit uneasily with the inclusiveness of the stories about recovery of the lost.

There are admittedly different emphases here, and the balance is different in different Gospels. Matthew is stronger on separating out; Luke is stronger on inclusiveness. Using psychological terminology, Matthew's thinking has more 'splitting' and lower 'integrative complexity' than Luke's.

It is hard to be sure which is more faithful to Jesus, but I can make sense of both strands if I take recovery of the lost as primary. Recovering the lost, and bringing everything together to restore wholeness, is not easily achieved. It may be necessary to make some hard choices to achieve it. Perhaps wholeness (and recovery of the lost) is the supreme goal for which other things have to be set aside, with a clear sense of priorities.

*Question:*

*Does what Jesus says about recovery of the lost have an emotional impact on you?*

## Light and Dark in Jesus' Life

The story of Jesus' life illustrates in a remarkable way how light and dark are intertwined. There are light and dark aspects of every key story. However, this is not always obvious in the way the events in Jesus' life are commemorated. There is often a tendency towards 'splitting', and to seeing particular events in Jesus' life as being all good or all bad. In contrast, I want to say that everywhere you look in Jesus' life you find good and bad elements jostling together. I think it is really important to recognise this, as the annual commemoration of particular events in the life of Jesus can then do more to help each one of us in our journey towards personal integration.

Let us start with Christmas, still much the most popular Christian festival, even if the celebration of it is often not particularly religious. Every other Christian festival is widely ignored, but almost everyone takes notice of Christmas in some way or other. No one can get through December without hearing a carol about a baby born in a manger. For most people Christmas is purely festivity, but the actual Christmas story, if you stop to think about it, is a remarkable integration of darkness and light.

In Luke's well-known version of the story, a heavily pregnant woman is forced by an occupying power to take a difficult journey with Joseph to her home town for a census. On arrival, she gave birth but, as there was no accommodation, her infant child had to be placed in a manger. Matthew says less about the birth itself, but has a dark story about how Herod, in an effort to kill Jesus, slaughtered every infant in Bethlehem. Jesus was only spared because his parents had been warned to escape as refugees to Egypt. This is not obviously a cause for celebration.

There are some brighter elements too, focusing largely on visitors. Luke has a story about shepherds on the hillside seeing angels, and Matthew has one about wise men from the East bringing presents. But the bright side of the story comes largely from the Christian interpretation of dark events as marking a decisive turn for the better in the human story.

Taken together, the story is a paradigm of the integration of light and dark, of how good things can arise from very adverse circumstances. Maybe it is some dim awareness of that intermingling of adversity and hope that makes the Christmas story so popular, even if the celebrations of most people now largely ignore what is being celebrated.

This theme of the intermingling of light and darkness is a feature of almost every key event in Jesus' life. The story of Jesus is as far removed from a compartmentalisation into light and darkness as any story could be; indeed it seems to be a protest against that kind of splitting into black and white.

That is true of the story of Jesus' baptism, which is partly an uplifting story about Jesus coming up out of the river and seeing the heavens open and the Spirit of God coming to rest on him. The sting comes in the tail, with Jesus going off into the wilderness for forty days of fasting and temptation.

There is a similar conjunction of light and dark in the story of Jesus' 'transfiguration'. His three closest followers see him shining with a bright light, and hear a voice from the sky saying, 'This is my beloved Son.' But the story comes shortly after Jesus saying that he will go to Jerusalem and that he will be put to death there, and it is followed shortly by another repetition of that prediction.

There is a similar intermingling of light and dark when Jesus arrives in Jerusalem. In some ways it is a hero's entry, riding into the city with cheering crowds. But he rides only on a donkey, which is a conspicuously lowly beast. Once in the centre of Jerusalem, the mood soon becomes confrontational, and the cheering evaporates and turns into a demand for Jesus to be crucified.

Crucifixion itself is a terrible way to die, and this is a very dark story indeed. But it is lightened by what Jesus says and does on the cross. In Luke, Jesus shows forgiveness of one of the criminals being crucified with him; in John, he shows his concern for his mother. As Thomas Kelly's hymn puts it, 'Inscribed upon the cross we see, in shining letters, *God is love*'.

The Easter story of Resurrection is actually a darker story than you would realise from most Easter services. The first intimation of Jesus' Resurrection comes to Mary while she is distraught and in tears outside the empty tomb. In Luke's version, the male disciples remain terrified and confused, huddled in a locked room, until the evening. It is a story of the gradual alleviation of grief and fear.

I feel that Christians sometimes obscure this intermingling of light and darkness by making Good Friday all gloom and Easter Day all joy. Neither is altogether convincing, either to the Bible story or to the realities of human life. The Easter Vigil service, for those who go, is more faithful to the complexity of the story in starting (literally) in darkness, and gradually moving through to celebration.

If our personal stories are placed alongside the complexity of the story of Jesus, it provides resources to help us to hold things together. Most people struggle, at least on occasions, with difficult events. In coping with them it helps to retain some good memories and some hopes for the future. Most people also have times of celebration, but they can seem frothy and ephemeral if they simply ignore problems and difficulties; then they become just some kind of escapism.

> *Question:*
>
> *How easily can you hold together the light and the dark in stories about Jesus, such as Christmas and Easter?*

## Beliefs About Jesus

Church people have been very concerned with what people believe about Jesus, but it is worth noting that, according to the Gospels, Jesus is not concerned with that. He hardly ever makes claims about himself nor, for the most part, seems concerned with what people think about him.

The notable exception, just before the disciples see Jesus transfigured with a bright light, is when Jesus asks his disciples who they think he is (Matthew 16:13–20). Peter says that Jesus is the Messiah, but Jesus just says he should tell no one. Jesus does not seem in the least concerned about whether or not people think he is God.

The various titles used about Jesus are all somewhat inconclusive and, for the most part, do not clearly say what most Christians now believe, that Jesus was actually God. Jesus sometimes calls himself the 'Son of Man' but that means a representative human, not that he is God.

To say that Jesus is the 'Son' of God is also more ambiguous than is sometimes realised, and probably just means that there is an identity of purpose between Jesus and the Father. To say that Jesus is the Christ or the Messiah just means that Jesus is the anointed one that God had promised Israel. In one of the clearest doctrinal statements in the New Testament, Peter says that Jesus was 'singled out' by God and 'attested to' through his miracles (Acts 2:22). That stops a long way short of saying that Jesus *was* God, it actually sits more easily with the idea that Jesus was adopted by God.

My point here is not to argue against conventional beliefs about Jesus, but just to point out, if people find them troublesome, that they are having problems with what later Christians have claimed about Jesus rather than with what the Bible says. If Christians were simply more 'biblical' about Jesus, they would create fewer obstacles to Christian allegiance.

The New Testament is more decisive about what Jesus achieved through his death and Resurrection, and I think that is the right place to put the emphasis. Apart perhaps from Mark, all New Testament writers regard the death and Resurrection of Jesus as supremely important. However, the claim, especially in the Acts of the Apostles, is that 'God raised him up' (Acts 2:32) rather than that Jesus rose of his own accord because he was God.

The deep conviction that runs through the New Testament is that Jesus brings about a decisive change in the prospects for humanity through his death and Resurrection, and that he has blazed a trail that others can follow. As we said earlier, there is no settled view about how that has been achieved. Various different ideas jostle together in the New Testament, and still do. But there seems no doubt at all that the New Testament writers, especially Paul, were convinced that, through Jesus, something had changed decisively for humanity.

One continuing debate among Christians is about whether things have changed for all humanity, or just for Christian believers. It is really both. My own sympathies are with the view that they have changed for everyone, and I think that is the implicit background assumption of the New Testament. The claim is that, because of Jesus, there is a new humanity. Of course, it is still useful for individuals to align themselves with what Jesus has done, but I don't think that is the starting point. In the next chapter, I will look at ideas about how Jesus might have been a turning point in human evolution.

> *Question:*
> *What do you believe about Jesus?*

## Bible Study

If you have time, it would be worth reading one of the Gospels again in full, and to read it as far as possible with fresh eyes. Different people have different favourite Gospels. The first three 'synoptic' Gospels overlap a good deal. Some like Mark, as the shortest and earliest of the Gospels. I personally like Luke, as the Gospel that puts most emphasis on compassion and inclusivity. There is also too much value in John, the most spiritually reflective of the Gospels.

If a whole Gospel is too much, the section in Luke between the transfiguration and the entry to Jerusalem includes many gems (Luke 9:28–19:28). I have focused here especially on Luke 15. That includes the story of the lost sheep; the core of the story is also found in Matthew 18:12–14, and is elaborated in a different way in John 10:1–18.

It is also instructive to read the proclamation about Jesus in the Acts of the Apostles (2:14–42); notice what is *not* said, as well as what is said about Jesus.

## Background and Sources

Geza Vermes (1981) *Jesus the Jew.* Augsburg Fortress. Vermes is a distinguished Jewish scholar who 'gets' Jesus better than most Christians.

Werner Pelz (1963) *God is No More.* Victor Gollancz. Pelz has helped me more than anyone else to hear the words of Jesus in their challenging freshness.

Stephen Verney (1995) *Water into Wine: An Introduction to John's Gospel.* Darton, Longman & Todd. A profound and beautifully written guide to the journey of personal transformation in the fourth Gospel.

Neil Douglas-Klotz (1999) *The Hidden Gospel: Decoding the Spiritual Message of the Aramaic Jesus.* Quest Books. Uses knowledge of the language Jesus spoke to get behind the language in which the Gospels were written.

Edward F. Edinger (1991) *Ego and Archetype: Individuation and the Religious Function of the Psyche.* Shambhala Publications. A Jungian reading of Jesus as a prophet of individuation.

Stevan L. Davies (1995) *Jesus the Healer: Possession, Trance and the Origins of Christianity.* SCM Press. Understands the centrality of healing in the life of Jesus, and approaches it with the help of recent work in the human sciences.

Jan-Olav Henriksen and Karl Olav Sandnes (2016) *Jesus as Healer: A Gospel for the Body.* W. B. Eerdmans. A somewhat cautious but thorough and workmanlike study of Jesus as healer.

James D. G. Dunn (1989) *Christology in the Making: A New Testament Inquiry into the Origins of the Doctrine of the Incarnation.* 2nd edition. SCM Press. A classic study of the titles accorded Jesus in the New Testament.

John W. Miller (1997) *Jesus at Thirty: A Psychological and Historical Portrait.* Fortress Press. A psychological study of the life and personality of Jesus.

Fraser Watts (ed.) (2007) *Jesus and Psychology.* Templeton Press. This is my own book on Jesus; it considers the role of psychology in understanding Jesus and studying the Gospels.

# Chapter Twelve
## *Sin and Salvation*

## What Difference Does Jesus Make?

I have claimed that beliefs about what Jesus accomplished are more central to Christianity than beliefs about whom he was. That may surprise some people, but I am confident that it is a fair reflection of the New Testament position. Having made that claim, I now need to try to explain as best I can how Jesus might have made fundamental changes to the human condition, perhaps to the whole of Creation.

Some people might say that it is when people *believe* in Jesus that he makes a difference, but it seems that makes what Jesus accomplished too dependent on subjective human responses. It may be helpful to imagine a hypothetical situation in which no one knew about the Resurrection of Jesus, and no one believed in the risen Jesus. Would that mean that nothing had changed, and that Jesus' death and Resurrection had achieved nothing? I think the Christian belief (and my own) is that things would have changed radically, whether or not anyone knew about it or believed in it.

At the heart of Christianity is the belief that Christ, through his death and Resurrection, did something decisive to help humans to find their freedom. Christians have expressed that in various ways, but no single idea about it seems to capture it completely. So, various ideas have been used alongside each other, each of which seems to capture something important, even if it doesn't say everything.

Which idea seems most compelling may depend on what kind of people we are. For example, if we are feeling anxious and feeling threatened, it may mean a lot to us that Christ has won a victory over the dark forces of sin and death. Or, if we feel guilty, it may mean a lot to us that Christ, innocent though he was, has taken the punishment that we deserve for our wrongdoing. Many people have been moved by the sacrificial love they see Jesus showing on the cross, and have been encouraged by it to lead better lives themselves. As Isaac Watts' well-known hymn puts it: 'Love so amazing, so divine demands my soul, my life, my all.'

While there is much that is true and helpful in these ancient ideas, it may be useful to develop some modern ideas alongside them, to help us to understand the great mystery of how Christ has liberated humanity through his death and Resurrection. The fact that several different ideas jostle together in the Bible and through Christian history gives us some freedom to develop new ideas, alongside the old ones. That is what I want to try to do here.

As I have done throughout this book, I will draw on ideas from psychology and weave them together with ideas from religion and spirituality. I don't want to claim that the ideas about the work of Christ that I will sketch out here provide a completely adequate explanation of what he accomplished. But I hope they add something useful to the rich ideas that we have inherited.

Most ideas about what Jesus accomplished make some reference to 'sin' and claim that, in some way, Jesus dealt with the problems of sin. So I need to spend part of this chapter exploring what 'sin' is. Like other key words in Christian thinking, it is often misunderstood. As we saw in chapter eight, the words 'repent' and 'forgive' sound much more negative than the Greek words they translate, and they probably don't really convey what Jesus meant. The same is true of the word 'sin', which has very negative connotations. So first we need to clear away the off-putting connotations that have gathered around that word and get back to what it really means.

*Question:*

*Does it make sense to you to claim that Jesus made a permanent and decisive difference to us all?*

# The Concept of Sin

For most people, 'sin' implies things that are disapproved of. Sins are thought of as things that we would like to do, because they are actually rather fun, things that are basically pretty harmless, *but* which are disapproved of, and which we come under strong pressure not to do.

Most of us carry around the idea that some things we do, or would like to do, are disapproved of. It is an idea that develops in childhood as we internalise the prohibitions of our parents. This inner sense of things being disapproved of develops during the 'superego'; it can be strict, cross, constraining and punishing. All this has very little connection with the Christian idea of sin, especially as we find it in the teaching of Jesus. Most people need to radically rethink what 'sin' means, because it is not what they thought it was.

We can start with the New Testament word for sin, which means 'falling short', falling short of the glory of God, of his dream of what we might be, and of the dance of love that is at the heart of God. More specifically, it means 'missing the mark', which is a metaphor that comes from archery. It means aiming for the bullseye, but not hitting it. An English word that captures well what sin really means is 'misguided'. Sinful actions are literally misguided in the sense that they take us off course in relation to where we are trying to get to.

The important point here is that sin is not all bad; there is often something well-intentioned about it. In sin we are often aiming for something worthwhile, but going about it in the wrong way. If there are things in your life that you feel are sinful, it is worth asking what you are trying to achieve and how else you might try to reach your goal.

This brings us to another important corrective to the connotations that the word 'sin' has for many of us. We assume that what we want to do is being blocked by moral disapproval and prohibition. We almost imagine that sin would be good for us, or at least it would be fun, if only we were left free to get on with it. On the contrary, sin is, by definition, what works *against* our best interests. Of course we can easily be short-sighted about what is in our best interests and go for things that bring short-term satisfaction, even if they work against our best long-term interests. Avoiding sin is about avoiding things that work against our best long-term interests.

If God wants us to avoid sin, it is because God wants the best for us and is on our side. God is not a killjoy who wants to stop us having fun. If we join with God in wanting what is truly best for us, it will bring us closer to God.

*Question:*
*How will it help you if you avoid 'sin'?*

## Hard and Soft Sins

Though sin can be anything that works against our best interests, and against God's benign purposes for us, there are some things that often lead us astray and would feature in any list of common sins. They fall into two main groups, that we might call 'soft' and 'hard' sins.

Soft sins include various ways in which we like to indulge ourselves: physical comforts, food and drink, sensual pleasures and so on. Soft sins are warm and comforting. Some Christians have tried to avoid those things entirely, though most think there is nothing wrong with them in moderation, and provided they don't become our overwhelming priority. However, indulgence can easily become addictive.

Soft sins are often linked to a weakness of character that can leave us struggling to find the commitment to do the things that are most important to us. There is a new scientific interest in 'willpower' and how it works. It seems that we can build up our willpower by exercising it, rather like a muscle. Willpower gets stronger with use; too much indulgence can weaken it, and soft sins weaken us.

Hard sins, in contrast, are cold and callous. They are built around our sense of power and importance and our desire to be in control. They bring out our pride and arrogance and can lead us to treat other people with insensitivity, or even cruelty. We can come to see other people as pawns in our game, not as people who are important in their own right.

For God, everyone is important in their own right. God never falls into the trap of making one person subordinate to the needs of another. Everyone has a place in God's purposes. God is also exquisitely sensitive to each person, to their joys and sorrows. Treating other people with insensitivity takes us a long way from how God relates to them, and distances us from God.

Hard and soft sins seem to be opposite, but actually there can often be an unholy alliance between them. We can be both callous towards others and indulgent towards ourselves at the same time. The common thread is *egocentricity*, the tendency to get so locked into our own needs and desires that we become almost indifferent to other people.

Egocentricity is probably the modern word that comes closest in meaning to sin. It means getting so wrapped up in our own point of view and our own desires that we can't see beyond them. It is egocentricity that separates us from God and other people, egocentricity that leads us to treat other people badly, egocentricity that leads us to prioritise our own short-term desires over what is actually best for us and for others.

The word 'sin' is used frequently in Christian circles. You might like to try replacing it, whenever it occurs, with 'egocentricity', and see if that is helpful. It is too long a word to trip off the tongue easily, but I think it captures very well what we mean by 'sin'. We all stand in need of deliverance from our egocentricity.

What is to be done about sin, about the human tendency to be egocentric, short-sighted, overindulgent and hard-hearted? If we know what is best for us, we will want to be free of all that. But how can that happen?

*Question:*

*How will it help you if you avoid 'sin'?*

## Jesus as a Turning Point in Human Evolution

I think we are better able now to describe the difference Jesus made than were people in Jesus' own time, partly because we can bring to that task what we now understand about human evolution. Already in Darwin's time, attempts were being made to place Christ in the context of human evolution. One obvious idea is that Jesus represents a culmination of one phase of evolution. Eventually, evolution gave rise to a species (humans) in which it was possible for Jesus to have a special sense of connection with the Father, and for Jesus' contemporaries to believe in him the way they did.

More speculatively, it is possible to suggest that Jesus initiated a new and more spiritual phase of evolution. That is not a belief that every Christian would hold, but to some, like Pierre Teilhard de Chardin, it has seemed compelling. However, even if this idea is accepted, there remains the question of exactly how Jesus initiated this new phase in human evolution, and why he was needed. Couldn't it just have happened anyway? I want to develop ideas about Jesus in relation to human evolution that place him more clearly as a turning point.

I suggest that Jesus initiated a process of inner spiritual renewal of humanity, 'from the inside out', so to speak. Some centuries before Jesus, people had had a vivid sense of God being active through nature; hailstones were seen as an expression of God's anger etc. This thinking can be found in the Psalms, for example. It is often called 'animism'. But some centuries before Jesus, this way of experiencing God had begun to fade and, if the process had continued, could have left humanity with no experience of God at all.

The sense of God speaking through particular people, known as prophets, also seems to have faded. With Old Testament prophets like Amos, there is a strong sense of their just being a mouthpiece for the word of God. They seemed to have been so possessed by God that the words they spoke were felt to be identical with what God was saying. Though people can still cultivate a sense of God speaking to them, it no longer happens with the power and immediacy characteristic of the Old Testament prophets. That fading of the prophetic consciousness also seems to have happened before the time of Jesus.

I suggest that Jesus initiates a new mode of spirituality that replaces the old animistic, prophetic consciousness. Jesus seems to have had a deep concern with inner spirituality. I suggest that his goal was to give humanity a new experience of the spirit dwelling within people, making his 'home' with them, as John's Gospel puts it. Looked at in this way, Pentecost, the gift of the Spirit, is the goal and purpose of Jesus' work. On this view, Jesus marks a turning point in the relation of humanity, nature and spirit, and makes that turning point possible.

The claim, made for example by Owen Barfield, is that before Jesus, humanity experienced spirit as coming from outside and speaking through nature. After Jesus, spirit is experienced within. Rather than spirit speaking to humanity through nature, there is a new possibility of humans looking at nature with spirit-imbued eyes. Barfield presents evidence from the study of how words have changed their meanings to support this view of a significant turning point in the evolution of human consciousness that coincided with Jesus.

The new consciousness that Jesus initiated is reflected in a new approach to morality that puts the emphasis on where people are coming from, on their thoughts and desires as much as on their actual behaviour. In the Sermon on the Mount, Jesus makes this point very explicitly in relation to murder and adultery Matthew 5:21–30). I think Jesus was quite innovative in how he saw moral renewal working itself out in practice, in a way that reflected his new emphasis on inner spirituality.

A similar idea of Jesus as a turning point in human development can be reached by taking Jung's ideas about how an individual human develops, and extrapolating them to the development of humanity. Jung considers that the first half of life is importantly different from the second, and that there is a mid-life turning point. He sees the first half of life as growing up from birth, and the second as moving towards death.

The tasks of the first half of life require the development of the ego as a distinct centre of consciousness. The second half of life requires the ego to reconnect with the 'Self', which is the whole personality that we have the potential to become, and the image of God in the psyche. To make that transition possible, the 'Self' needs to reach out to the ego. In a similar way, one could say that God needs to reach out to humanity. That is one way of understanding what God was doing in Jesus.

*Question:*

*Does it make sense to you that Jesus changed the course of human development?*

## Photosynthesis as a Metaphor for the Work of Christ

Now, I want to suggest that photosynthesis provides a helpful metaphor for what Jesus did at his crucifixion. Photosynthesis is the process by which plants convert light into energy that they can use; it involves absorbing carbon dioxide from the environment and emitting oxygen. Many people are familiar with it from school biology. I suggest, by analogy, that Christ has changed the moral spiritual air we breathe, as plants change the physical atmosphere by photosynthesis.

The first research on photosynthesis was carried out by Joseph Priestley. He found that if a candle was lit in an airtight container, the flame soon extinguished; a mouse died if it was put in an airtight container in which a candle had burned out. However, he found that the mouse was able to live if a plant was placed inside the airtight container. Putting a sprig of mint or some other plant in an airtight jar in which a candle had burned out restored the 'injured' air, enabling the mouse to live. The plant absorbed carbon dioxide and released oxygen, giving the mouse the oxygen it needed for life.

My analogy is that the moral and spiritual air that humans breathe has become injured by too much fear and hatred being released into it. That injures the atmosphere in a way that is analogous to how carbon dioxide injures the atmosphere. If nothing is done to restore the atmosphere, animal life becomes impossible.

Just as plants absorb the carbon dioxide that poisons the atmosphere and release the oxygen that restores it, so I suggest that what Jesus does on the cross is to absorb the huge fear and hatred that was misdirected towards him, resulting in his crucifixion; he converts it into love and compassion that heals the moral and spiritual atmosphere.

Jesus is like the sprig of mint in Priestley's experiment that healed the injured atmosphere and enabled the mouse to live. He was able to do this because of his extraordinary capacity to absorb fear and hatred, without feeling fear and hatred himself in response. It provides a model for how other people can try to heal the injured moral and spiritual atmosphere around them. On the cross, Christ exposed himself to the worst that humans can do and soaked up all that he was exposed to, as a plant absorbs carbon dioxide. Christ then transformed it into the oxygen of love that can support life. Inspired by Christ, we too can soak up fear and hatred and breathe out love.

Such analogies are never exact, but I think science provides a useful source of analogies that help to make sense of Christian belief. Photosynthesis provides a helpful extra way of thinking about how good came from Jesus' crucifixion.

*Question:*

*Does it make sense to you that Jesus,*
*on the cross, soaked up*
*all human negativity and transformed it?*

# Jesus as a Scapegoat:
# A Metaphor from Family Systems Theory

Now I will turn to a metaphor from family systems theory and suggest that Jesus plays a role for humanity that is analogous to the role of a scapegoat in the family. I am not actually advocating this understanding of what Jesus does on the cross, but I think the analogy helps to clarify some of the implicit assumptions in the idea that Jesus paid the price for the sin of humanity.

As we have come to understand better how families function, it has become clear that sometimes, if one person suffers or becomes ill, it enables others to remain happy and healthy. There is something similar in how Christ suffers to enable humanity to have life and health. The scapegoat usually gets blamed for everything that goes wrong in the family, including many things that are not his or her fault. That takes the pressure off other family members, because it protects them from being blamed for what they have done.

For example, a child may play the scapegoat for her or his parents, enabling them to get on better, without blaming each other. Sometimes the scapegoat gets ill and suffers in that way, rather than by being blamed. The crucial role of the scapegoat in enabling others to flourish is apparent if the scapegoat ceases to play that role. That often makes it impossible for other family members to continue to flourish.

The family scapegoat is an innocent who takes the blame. That is very damaging for the scapegoat, but very helpful for the rest of the family. The analogy with the Christian understanding of the crucifixion of Jesus is clear. Jesus is the innocent who suffers, in a way that benefits others. This kind of thinking is deeply ingrained in the thinking of the ancient Jewish people, when an innocent animal was slaughtered to atone for the wrongdoing of the whole people.

Though the analogy between Jesus and a family scapegoat works in some respects, there are some significant differences. Jesus accepts the role of scapegoat more knowingly and willingly than is normal in family dynamics. However, scapegoating remains a dysfunctional process. Even if Jesus takes on the scapegoat role willingly and in a spirit of self-sacrifice, he is still, on this model, colluding with a dysfunctional process rather than healing it.

It is also not clear that the mechanism by which family members benefit from having a scapegoat works for the whole human race, or at least not in the same way. Family systems theory is sometimes extended to communities, but the process of shifting blame that is involved seems to require a tightly knit community, and that doesn't seem to be the case with Jesus and humanity.

> *Question:*
> *Do you find it helpful to think of Jesus as a scapegoat?*

## How We Benefit

Though Christians believe that Christ has done something decisive through his death and Resurrection, there are further issues about how the benefits of that work themselves out. Clearly, two thousand years on, many things are still difficult on the ground. Why is that?

As I see it, Christ has created opportunities, but we need to take those opportunities. It is Christ and us together that can reap the benefits. It requires collaboration. We can't leave it all to him, but neither can we do it all ourselves. We can do it together. For that to work, we need to develop a strong connection with Christ; we need to be, as St Paul puts it, 'in Christ'.

Human weakness and egocentricity (or 'sin') can keep us trapped in what feels like a prison; we go on making the same mistakes over and over again. Sin is rather compulsive; we seem to be in its grip. We often seem powerless to break free. That is an experiential reality for many people; it is not just abstract doctrine.

Through a close relationship with Christ, we can find the extra resources we need to break free. We find in practice that if we are 'in Christ', we can get further than if we are trying to go it alone. Up to a point, this works in a way that is similar to how any close friendship would work. With Christ, we have someone who is stronger and wiser than us, more clear-sighted than we are, and who wants the best for us. If we stay close to him we get through better, and are less likely to 'miss the mark', or to slip into the misguided actions that constitute sin.

But there are also special features of our relationship with Christ that set it apart from even the most supportive human relationship. For one thing, Christ is an unseen companion, but he is always present; we can tune in to him whenever we need to. There are many ways of doing that. We encounter him in those around us, especially those in need, as his story of the sheep and goats says. We can also find him in prayer and worship, and in reading about him in the Gospels. When we tune in to Christ, we connect with his great work on the cross of transforming fear and hatred into love and healing. We participate in that great work, across the divide of time and space, and find ourselves being drawn into it and benefiting from it.

As we get drawn into this great project we find freedom; we experience a liberation from the misguided tendencies that so easily operate within us. We get liberation from the limitations and twistedness that work against our own best interests, and the best interests of those around us. Then we can experience what St Paul called the 'glorious liberty of the children of God' (Romans 8:21).

> *Question:*
>
> *How could you align yourself*
> *more closely with the benefits of Jesus'*
> *death and Resurrection?*

## Bible Study

The idea of the sacrificial lamb bearing the iniquities of the people is an important one in the Old Testament, and has shaped Christian thinking about the work of Christ, see Leviticus 16:7–22. As I have suggested, it seems that one member of a dysfunctional family can play a somewhat similar role.

For an example of animistic thinking about nature in the Old Testament, see Psalm 18:6–19. Elijah comments on his not finding God in this way but in the sound of sheer silence (1 Kings 19:11–13). The most vivid account of a prophet being singled out by God, and told what to say, is in the first few chapters of Ezekiel (e.g. Ezekiel 2:1–7). By the end of the Old Testament, prophets are not just in decline, but disapproved of (Zechariah 13:2–6).

John's Gospel has a strong sense of the spirit within as a gift of Jesus, for example in what Jesus says to the Samaritan woman about springs of living water welling up within (John 4:14) and about the Spirit coming to dwell within (John 14:10 and 17).

Though St Paul has a strong sense of the importance of believing in Jesus Christ, and of living as children of light, this is based on a clear belief in Christ as a kind of new 'Adam', (i.e. new humanity). 'As in Adam all die, so in Christ shall all be made alive' (1 Corinthians 15:22 and 45).

## Background and Sources

On rethinking the concept of sin, see Stephen Verney (1989) *The Dance of Love*. Collins. What I say here about hard and soft sins is influenced by Rudolf Steiner's approach to evil, on which see Bernard Nesfield-Cookson (1983) *Rudolf Steiner's Vision of Love*. Aquarian Press. Chapter nine. For recent research on willpower see Roy F. Baumeister and John Tierney (2012) *Willpower: Why Self-Control is the Secret to Success*. Penguin.

On psychological approaches to the doctrine of atonement see Fraser Watts, Rebecca Nye and Sara Savage (2002) *Psychology for Christian Ministry*. Routledge. pp. 290–94.

Probably the best book putting Christ in evolutionary context is Gerd Theissen (1984) *Biblical Faith: An Evolutionary Approach*. SCM Press (republished by Fortress Press in 2000). I have written more myself about Christ in evolutionary context in Fraser Watts (2002) *Theology and Psychology*. Ashgate. Chapter nine.

On the fading of prophetic consciousness see Julian Jaynes (1976) *The Origin of Consciousness in the Breakdown of the Bicameral Mind*. Allen Lane. Chapter eight (though I think he gets the neuroscience back to front, as I explain in Fraser Watts and Léon Turner (eds.) (2014) *Evolution, Religion and Cognitive Science*. Oxford University Press).

For Owen Barfield's approach to Christ in evolutionary context see Owen Barfield (1957) *Saving the Appearances: A Study in Idolatry*. Faber & Faber. For a Jungian approach, see Edward Edinger (1977) *Ego and Archetype: Individuation and the Religious Function of the Psyche*. Pelican.

As far as I know there is no previous literature on the metaphors for the work of Christ I have drawn from photosynthesis and family systems theory. For general background see Torrey Maloof (2015) *Photosynthesis*. Teacher Created Materials, and Eia Asen (1995) *Family Therapy for Everyone*. BBC Books.

# Chapter Thirteen
## *God Beyond Words*

## What Do We Mean by 'God'?

Finally, at the end of our journey, we come to God. What do we mean by 'God'? In chapter nine I claimed that there is a widespread intuition that there is something more, call it God or not. Many people have a sense that this something more is connected with truth, beauty and goodness and is also relational, intimate and caring. I also mentioned some lines of work in modern science that support the view that there is something more than space-time, something more than matter. However, I have largely postponed until now whether we want to call this something more 'God', and what it means to do so.

There are many ways of trying to understand the idea of God in Christianity (and I am talking here about the classical tradition, not about what might be easily dismissed as watered down, modern 'liberalism'). There are misunderstandings about the idea of 'God', both among believers and non-believers. People often cling to ways of understanding God that make the idea of God more difficult than it need be. I want to say that believing in God really doesn't have to be that difficult!

First, I have some ground clearing to do. I will talk first, not so much about what we mean by 'God', as about what we *don't* mean by 'God'. There is nothing newfangled or wishy-washy about this;

there is a venerable tradition of Christian theology, sometimes called 'negative theology', that sees the main task as learning what we *can't* say about God. The main obstacle to calling the something more 'God' comes from misleading (or at least unnecessary) ideas about God. I will first try to clear these obstacles out of the way, and then to speak more positively about what we mean by God.

Most atheists seem to have a very simplistic idea of God, which makes little sense and is hard to accept. They perhaps have a vested interest in keeping an idea of God going that is so incredible that there is good reason to reject it. However, there is a huge gap between the God that atheists reject and the God of thoughtful Christians. The God that atheists reject is usually one that no thoughtful Christian would believe in anyway.

But, even among believers, there is often something problematic about the idea of God. Over the years I have found that there is an increasing number of people who are struggling with the idea of God, or at least with the God that they thought they were supposed to believe in. It is something that makes many people wonder whether they can, with integrity, be Christian at all. But again, this need not be as big a problem as is often imagined.

We lack a good empirical survey of ways of referring to God (or the divine), but there are some for whom the traditional, rather anthropomorphic language is unproblematic, and others for whom it is impossible. However, given the inadequacy of all ways of thinking about God, I think we should be more welcoming and inclusive of a variety of ways of thinking about God, such as God is the 'deepest reality of all', or God is 'pure love'.

There is a clue to the nature of the problem in survey research, which shows that the number of people who believe in God is significantly higher than the number who believe in a 'personal' God. It seems that there is a substantial number of people who believe in God, in some sense, but not in a 'personal' God. Put like that, it may seem a very unorthodox position, but I don't think that is necessarily so. The kind of personal God that many people reject is a God created too much in the image of a human being. It is, you might say, a rather 'anthropomorphic' God. Our idea of God is often too small, too limited, too constrained by our human habits of thought.

We seem to have come up with an idea of God who is some kind of superhuman being, albeit one who has extraordinary powers and characteristics, altogether unlike those of any human being. The two sides of this anthropomorphic God don't easily go together; they seem a contradiction in terms. It doesn't make sense to many people to have a God who is really rather like a human being, but who is also utterly transcendent and supernatural. Faced with this problem, it seems clear that what should go is the habit of thinking about God as rather like a human being. Apart from God's revelation of himself in Jesus, God is nothing like a human being.

Bishop John Robinson, author of *Honest to God*, put this in a catchy way fifty years ago in a headline in a Sunday newspaper: 'God is not a Daddy in the Sky'. Quite so. You might say that no Christian ever thought that God was a daddy in the sky. But the idea of God that is associated with Christianity is uncomfortably close to a 'daddy in the sky'. At the very least, Christians have allowed people to think that is what they believe in. It would really help if Christians said more clearly that it is not what they believe.

For many people, the word 'God' has become a problem; not the reality of God, but the word. In the world of the Old Testament, the name of God, Yahweh, (Jehovah), was too sacred even to be uttered. The name itself is mysterious; it means something like 'I Am Who I Am'; it is certainly not like an ordinary human name. I rather admire the Jewish sense that the name of God is too sacred to be uttered. E. M. Forster referred to 'poor little talkative Christianity'; and he had a point. Christians could try talking less about God.

There are various advantages in this Biblical attitude of reverence to the name of God. One is that the word 'God' has come to have a lot of misleading overtones that get in the way of people experiencing the reality of God. Using the name less may actually help us to experience the reality of God better.

Some of the deepest religious experiences seem to be 'ineffable', i.e. they defy being put into words. I think there are several things that contribute to that sense of ineffability. One is that God is such a deep mystery that our human language isn't adequate for talking about God. To some extent that is also true of the reality in which there was no space and time from which the Big Bang emerged. Scientists can write equations about that world, but we can't really picture it or talk about it. We don't even quite know whether it is 'real', or quite what that would mean.

But with God, it is more than that. It is not just that he is a reality so different from our everyday world that our language can't really stretch to it. There is also something special about God. Many

Christians have often tried to say that, in one way or another. They say things like 'God reaches out to us and we respond, not vice versa', or 'God is a subject, not an object'. It is hard to find the right way to say it, but there is something important in this. God is not the kind of reality that we humans can pin down, so the path to a relationship with God needs to be based on humility.

> *Question:*
>
> *In what ways is God like a human person?*
>
> *How is he unlike a human person?*

## Words and Reality

We should be wary of anyone who claims to know too much about God, as they may be telling us about a God who is largely their own invention. It is only when we approach God humbly and reverently that we have a chance of experiencing the reality of God. There are different ways of thinking about that deepest reality of all that we call 'God'. However, as they are all ways of thinking about a reality that is beyond adequate human understanding, we should sit lightly on them all.

The most common way of thinking about God is as a person. That may be the best we can do, but it can become misleading if it suggests that God is rather like a human person, only bigger and better. We can't press the analogy between God and a human person too far. It is often when that analogy is taken too literally that people have trouble with the idea of 'God'.

Another way of thinking about God is as some kind of transcendent spiritual force or energy. That is not quite right either, as God is more personal and intimate than that. But for an increasing number of people it is a helpful first approximation in their journey into a relationship with God. It may be less misleading than thinking about him as too much like a human person.

Many Christians have realised that, as they grow deeper into God, they increasingly relate to him in silence. Words for God can be a crutch that we throw away as our relationship deepens. Because human words for God are all somewhat misleading, we can reach a point where we feel that words do more harm than good, and that it is better just to be silent in the presence of God.

We perhaps talk about God too much. The great anonymous work of medieval English mysticism, *The Cloud of Unknowing*, emphasised how limited our knowledge of God is: 'God may be well loved, but cannot be thought of. God may be reached and held close by means of love; but by means of thought never'. We can love God but we can't use our thinking to know God. Christians need to acknowledge more openly the strand of their tradition that recognises that all human language about God is bound to be hopelessly inadequate. In trying to think about God we are thinking at the boundaries of human thought.

Even if there is no change at all in the rather anthropomorphic language used about God in preaching and in liturgy, it would be a considerable help to those who find this language deeply problematic to hear a more open recognition that no human language is adequate when we talk about God. We talk about God as a person, and address him as such, partly just because there is no better language. However, we should acknowledge that God is not remotely comparable to other people. He is radically and incomparably different.

We talk about God as being all-knowing, all-powerful etc. That may sound like a description of God. Actually, I think it is more a way of putting down a marker that God is totally unlike a human being. We have rather limited cognitive capacity. God has no such limitations, which makes him completely unlike us.

For some time, people have been edging towards an alternative, more impersonal language for talking about God. Of major theologians in the last century, Paul Tillich addressed this issue most openly, with his suggestion that we think of God, not as a particular being, but as the ground of all being. I admit that I have never found the phrase 'ground of being' particularly helpful, but it can be taken as an example of a class of ways of referring to God. Variants that I find more user-friendly are Bishop John Robinson's God is the 'depth at the centre of life', or Bishop Stephen Verney's God is the 'deepest reality of all'. There are now many who think about God as a spiritual energy or force, or as a centre of consciousness or love.

It may well be the case that the two kinds of language suit different circumstances. I suspect that many people, under extreme stress, would pray to God using the old anthropomorphic language but who, in other circumstances, would use a more reflective and intellectual conceptualisation. There will also be differences between people, and some people will cope better with the latter kind of language than others. However, I suspect that the Christian Church tends to underestimate the number of people who, in some home-spun way, are already using a more impersonal way of thinking about God. I suspect that the faith of people in the pews is not quite as 'simple' as is often assumed, even if not very articulate.

There is also an increasing number of people who make some use of both ways of thinking about God, but sit light on both, because they recognise both as problematic and inadequate. There is also a third spiritual language, neither anthropomorphic nor impersonal, but silent. There has been a remarkable recent movement towards meditation and other silent forms of spirituality. Sadly, it is not widely appreciated that Christianity has a rich tradition of silent meditation and contemplative prayer, so many of those who want to learn to meditate go elsewhere.

Let us have more humility about all ways of thinking about God, and not give the impression that one is correct and the other is a watered-down sop. No way of thinking about God is adequate, though different ways of thinking about God have different deficiencies. There is a sound bite about praying that makes a lot of sense: 'Pray as you can, not as you can't.' I want to say something similar about thinking about God: 'Think about God as you can, not as you can't.'

*Question:*

*Do words and ideas about God sometimes get in the way of your experience of God?*

## God and Ourselves

There is a close connection between growing into a deeper relationship with God and finding our true selves. The two go together. That is not to equate God and ourselves. God is everything, 'all in all'. There cannot be anything at all that is not grounded in God; that is part of what the word 'God' means. We can find God through various different paths, through nature, through other people who inspire us, through social issues, and so on. But the journey into God and the journey into ourselves are closely intertwined. We can't do one without the other. We can't journey into a deeper relationship with God and bypass understanding ourselves better. Equally, if we go deeply and honestly into ourselves, we will find signs of God being at work there.

There seem to be layers in human personality. There is a surface layer where we need to operate much of the time, getting things done. But there is a deeper layer that influences much of what we do, even when we are not aware of it. That is where we find both the best and the worst of ourselves. Great progress was made in the twentieth century in understanding the deeper layers of personality, and we can use that wisdom to help us with the journey into God through ourselves.

Many people, if they are honest, find their personal journey somewhat disappointing. Some people live in circumstances that are objectively very difficult; but even those whose circumstances are relatively good often feel disappointed with life and with themselves. We may find that we don't really hang together as people, that we can be different people in different situations, with the result that we don't know whom we really are. Or we can find that our thinking, our feelings and our actions don't really line up together. Even St Paul complained that his actions often didn't match his intentions.

We may also find that, even when we are 'having a good time', it can feel a bit hollow. We may have looked forward to something for a long time but, when it comes, find it isn't all we had expected. Life can seem like wandering around in a desert, looking for a promised land that we never find.

If that matches your experience at all, you are well on the way to desiring God. If we are searching for the elusive centre that gives meaning and fulfilment to our lives, we are, in effect, searching for God, whatever we call it. Finding God is inseparable from finding whom we really are, finding how to live, finding fulfilment, finding meaning and purpose, finding the people God made us to be.

It is like searching for what Jesus called the 'kingdom of God'. As he said, that is like a very precious pearl for which it is worth setting everything else aside. It is crucial in the spiritual life to keep alive the hope, the dream, of finding that centre, that deep reality that makes sense of everything and brings true fulfilment.

The reality of God can break into our lives in a variety of ways (whether or not we recognise that reality as God, or call him that). There can be sudden moments of realisation, moments when we say, 'Aha, now I understand,' moments when things that have been puzzling us fall into place. At other times, moments of realisation creep up on us gradually.

It often arises from looking back over our lives and seeing things at work that we didn't understand at the time. It is often easier to see the hand of God at work when we look back. It is like the Old Testament story of Moses having to avert his gaze from the glory of God, because he couldn't look at God directly (Exodus 33:18–23). However, once God had passed by, he could turn and look at God's glory from behind.

It is not an accident that what is probably the first autobiography ever to be written was St Augustine's *Confessions,* in which he tells the story of how God had shaped him through his life. Discerning the spiritual story of our lives is a key part of the spiritual life, and something that can be helpful to all of us.

One useful exercise may be to imagine that your life is about to end, and that you have a chance to write a spiritual obituary of yourself. How would you tell the story? You might then go on to consider what story you would like to be able to tell about yourself if you could live a bit longer.

It may also be helpful to probe your desires, to try to understand why you want particular things. You may think it is obvious why you want things, but it can be very revealing to keep on asking, 'But why do I want that?'

You can also pay particular attention to those moments when things feel right, when you feel inspired, or when you feel you have come home to where you belong. Finding how God is at work in our lives can be like following a trail. There are moments when we feel we are 'getting warm'. If we linger over those moments, or go back to them, we can find the trail better.

Dreams can also be a helpful guide. We realise things about ourselves in dreams that we are not aware of in other ways. Not all dreams are rich and meaningful, but some are. There are many stories in the Bible of God speaking to people through dreams, and we too can encounter God through our dreams.

A Spanish Christian of the sixteenth century, St Teresa of Avila, wrote about her journey into God through the Self in a landmark book, *The Interior Castle.* She saw the journey as like going through a series of mansions in a castle until she came to the heart of the castle, where she found union with God.

In this journey, it is helpful to have maps to enable us to recognise landmarks and pitfalls. Prayer, the Scriptures, and sacraments such as Holy Communion, can all help to provide maps. It is also helpful to have as a spiritual guide someone who has been on this journey of finding God deep within us longer than we have and has found the way through.

> *Question:*
> *Are you aware of a deep layer in your personality*
> *that reflects God?*
> *How can you connect better with that aspect of yourself?*

## God and Desire

I have been trying here to establish the credibility of believing in the idea of 'God'. In a previous chapter, I looked at intuition that there is something more. Here, I have tried to deal with some widespread reservations about calling this something more 'God', and have tried to argue that those reservations are unnecessary. My main point is that the idea of God, when you get down to it, need not be as strange and difficult as many people assume. Let us set aside ideas about God that are not really faithful to the depth and richness of the Christian tradition. They trip up people who want to be Christians, which makes it easier to defend atheism.

Let us not be deterred from experiencing the reality of God in our personal journeys by narrow or misleading ideas about God. The reality of God is usually bigger and broader than our ideas about God. It is the reality of God that matters, not our human ideas about God.

When we meet a new person, we often want to know quite a lot about them. As we get to know them, we may weigh up what we think about them, whether we really like them, whether we want them as friends etc. We can't do that with God. We can't study God, evaluate God, and decide whether or not we want to be friends with God. We often like to be in charge in relationships, making the decisions. It doesn't work like that with God. The experience of people who have come to have a deep relationship with God is that God takes the initiative and we respond. It just doesn't happen the other way round.

There is usually an emotional quality to the experiences that bring us deeper into a relationship with God and our true selves. It is about desire, about being on a journey, about being drawn on towards some goal that we can't yet quite discern; it is about seeking and finding.

Most of our desires are for things we know and can identify. But this deep, ultimate desire that is best understood as a desire for God, is a desire for something or someone beyond us.

The journey may start with our desiring God. However, as we go deeper, it becomes more a matter of our being desired *by* God, desired by someone or something beyond ourselves. We come to know God, not as someone we can describe and talk about, but as a being who is beyond our full comprehension and who desires us as no one else does.

Another unusual thing about the relationship with God that makes it different from any human relationship is that God knows all about us. There is no hiding. We are generally quite selective over what we reveal about ourselves to other people; we generally try to keep up a good impression. But with God there is no scope for impression management. God sees everything.

That may seem alarming. We might assume that someone who knew everything about us could not possibly think well of us. The unique thing about God is that God knows everything, sees everything, but still loves us and desires us as no one else could, and wants the best for us. That is a moving, life-changing experience.

God also has hopes and dreams for us. God has a vision of the kind of people we might become, people who would experience deeper fulfilment than we can currently imagine. God helps us on that journey of personal transformation. God both points us in the right direction and supports us on the journey.

When we strip misleading words away, it is the reality and presence of God that we are left with. It is then the presence of God that we come to desire, not words or ideas about him. We long, as a modern worship song puts it, 'to be in your presence, to sit at your feet, where your love surrounds me and makes me complete'.

I end with a story told by Stephen Verney about when he asked a Greek abbot what really happened in prayer. The abbot said that there are three stages in prayer. First there is me and Him; then there is Him and me; and finally there is just Him.

*Question:*

*Where do your desires ultimately lead, if you follow them through? Do they lead to God?*

## Bible Study

Psalm 139:1–11, is a marvellous reflection on the presence of God, wherever a person might go.

St Paul talks about God being 'unsearchable', and calls for the 'renewing' of our minds (Romans 11:33–12:2), about the partial character of our current knowledge, which will be fulfilled in love (1 Corinthians 13:8–13), and about how we need the eyes of the heart to be enlightened if we are to understand the purposes of God (Ephesians 1:17–19).

You might like to read the story of Zacchaeus and Jesus (Luke 19:1–10) and compare his search for Jesus with your own search for God. Zacchaeus is curious and wants to see Jesus, but he doesn't want to get too close or be seen. But, in fact, Jesus does see him and takes the initiative.

## Background and Sources

One of the great classics of mystical Christianity is *The Cloud of Unknowing*, written anonymously in the fourteenth century. Another Christian classic is *The Interior Castle*, written by St Teresa of Ávila in 1577. For a psychological perspective on it see John Welch (1982) *Spiritual Pilgrims: Carl Jung and Teresa of Ávila*. Paulist Press.

The bestselling book that introduced many people to twentieth-century thinking about God was John Robinson (1963) *Honest to God*. SCM Press. See also Robinson's later book, *Truth is Two-Eyed*. SCM Press.

One of the best recent guides to debates about God is Keith Ward (2013) *God: A Guide for the Perplexed*. Oneworld Publications. For a multi-faith perspective see John Bowker (2014) *God: A Very Short Introduction*. Oxford University Press.

For a psychologically oriented guide to Tillich see Terry Cooper (2001) *Paul Tillich and Psychology*. Mercer University Press. On negative theology see Denys Turner (2009) *Faith Seeking*. SCM Press.

# Afterword
## *The Threefold Journey*
## *Towards Living More Deeply*

The journey through this book is almost over, but the journey of life goes on. My hope is that this book will provide resources to live the journey of life with greater spiritual depth. In chapter one I explained how this journey can be seen from the perspective of psychology on the one hand, and of religion and spirituality on the other. I urged that it is helpful to keep both perspectives in play, and that it is easier to see how best to live life more deeply, if you have both perspectives to guide you.

Now, finally, I want to see how the three aspects of living deeply represented by the three sections of this book relate to each other and help each other. Living deeply involves a new way of relating to the issues we face *ourselves* as we go through life, the challenges and opportunities we find in *others* and in events around us, and the ever-present call of that *deeper spiritual reality* that many call 'God'. The three facets of that transformation of our relationships are interrelated. They work together and each one helps the others. I will try to explain how that works.

Being true to oneself is the moral imperative of our age. It is the value that trumps all others. Whatever other virtues are on display are seen as almost worthless unless we are being genuine and sincere, and almost anything is permissible if we are being true to ourselves. This is very new. No other age has given such priority to authenticity. So there is no need to urge the importance of being true to oneself. We live in an age in which that is self-evident to everyone.

It all depends how you go about being true to yourself. Often people go about it in ways that are brash and superficial. In this book I have urged people to relate to themselves more deeply. Really being true to yourself is more difficult and demanding than people often seem to realise. The difference between shallow and deeper ways of being true to yourself is most evident when it comes to coping with stress, sadness, loss, illness and other forms of suffering.

You can use such hard times to grow in depth and genuineness. If you do that, your depth of personality will help you to cope with whatever personal difficulties come your way. If you relate to yourself in a way that is shallow and superficial you will not be able to cope. I am reminded of Jesus' story of two houses, one built on sand and the other on rock (Matthew 7:24–27). Only the house built on rock survived when storms came. Similarly, our way of being ourselves needs to have depth if it is to survive in difficult times.

You can't be yourself in isolation from other people. We are relational creatures. As the poet and priest John Donne famously put it, 'No man is an island, entire of itself.' We discover ourselves in relation to other people.

By being observant about how we react to others, we learn more about what kind of people we really are. Sometimes it is not good news. Altruistic behaviour is one example; research has shown that there are a lot of people who believe they are altruistic, but who do not help another person in need when the situation arises. On the other hand, the needs of others can sometimes bring out the best in us, and we surprise ourselves by how well we respond when other people need our help.

Sometimes people see things in us, whether good or bad, that we had not seen ourselves. Although in one sense we all know a lot about ourselves, our perspective can be blinkered or distorted, preventing us from seeing things that are obvious to other people. We can relate better to ourselves by doing it in the context of our relationships with other people.

Equally, if we are to relate well to other people, we need to be deeply rooted in ourselves. Though people can sometimes help us by seeing us more clearly than we can see ourselves, relationships with others can be confusing too. We can see in others what we want to see, not what is really there. Similarly, other people can project things on to us that arise from their own issues, but are not really there. This is very confusing and can destabilise us. It seems that the more people try to be of service to others and to relate to them at their point of deepest need, the more they are vulnerable to this kind of misunderstanding.

Working for forgiveness is a good example. Forgiveness and reconciliation are seldom straightforward. However well-intentioned they might be, anyone who works for them is open to misunderstanding. You have to have a deep and accurate understanding of yourself to be able to give and receive forgiveness, to work for forgiveness and reconciliation among others. If you have a shallow and distorted relationship to yourself, you will not be able to relate effectively to others when the going gets tough.

My point so far has been that relating well to yourself and relating well to others go hand in hand. You can't do one without the other. I want now to say that both are also intertwined with developing our relationship to deeper reality. As we go more deeply into ourselves, we find both good and evil there, and realise how interlocked they are. We find a divine spark within ourselves and realise that there is something of God at the core of ourselves (what Jung called the 'Self'); but we also discover how 'fallen' we are, and that we are dogged by a perverse tendency to fall short and miss the mark.

No journey inwards can fail to discover that a reflection of the deepest realities can be found within us. As we connect with these deep spiritual realities, we can learn to draw on what is life-giving and avoid what drags us down. In as far as we can do that, we will find that we are drawing on deep and powerful resources that will help us to relate better to ourselves and to others. These deeper realities are unavoidable in the journey to relate better to others, and the resources they provide are indispensable.

It is thus a threefold journey that involves relating better to ourselves, to others and to deeper realities. We may be tempted to try to follow one or even two of these paths on their own. In our own century, the big temptation is to try to relate better to ourselves, and to be more authentic, without concerning ourselves with how much we relate to others or to deeper spiritual realities. That simply doesn't work. Unless you are willing to pursue each aspect of this threefold journey, you will find you can't get very far with any one of them.

As I began to write this afterword, I realised that there was a strong convergence between what I wanted to say here (which is implicit in the three sections of this book), and what Stephen Verney says in his book *Into the New Age* (Collins, 1976) about a new way of relating to oneself, to others and to deeper reality. What I have written here is very much indebted to him, as so much else in this book has been. In chapter four of that book he explores this threefold path in relation to various examples. He sees Jesus himself as exemplifying this threefold renewal, and finds it also in the encounter of the Samaritan woman with Jesus (John 4).

Verney also sees forgiveness as exemplifying that threefold renewal and illustrates that with the story of Jesus' forgiveness of the paralysed man (Mark 2:3–12). The 'forgiveness of sins' involves the setting free of our true selves so that we can become the whole personality we have the potential to become and are called to be; for the paralysed man it meant that he could walk again. It also involves discovering the give and take of love that arises when people use forgiveness to release one another, and discover how interdependent they are; the paralysed man was very aware of how dependent he was on his friends to bring him to the house where Jesus was, and lower him through the roof to the feet of Jesus. As he met Jesus, he encountered the deep spiritual reality that shone out of him and felt the immense spiritual resources flowing through Jesus, and the paralysed man obeyed Jesus' command to walk again.

As you follow this threefold journey of renewal for yourself, may the Lord bless you and watch over you, make his face shine upon you, and look kindly on you and give you peace (Numbers 6:25–26).

# Living Deeply

Sections from this book are also available in a series of free YouTubes.
  Presenters: Roger Bretherton and Sara Savage.
  Film-maker: Nick Devenish.
  Each clip lasts c 4 minutes.
  They can be used for private viewing or group discussion.

For details and to download go to
  Cambridge Institute for Applied Psychology and Religion
  http://www.ciapr.co.uk/living-deeply/

## List of Film Clips

Module One
*Personal Issues*

1. Coping With Stress
    1.1. What stresses you?
    1.2. How to Cope
    1.3. How Support Can Help
    1.4. How Prayer Can Help

2. Getting Depressed
    2.1. Feeling Low
    2.2. Negative Thinking
    2.3. Getting Help
    2,4. The Spiritual Side of Depression

3. Loss and Death
    3.1. Being Bereaved
    3.2. The Silver Lining in Bereavement
    3.3. Know Your Feelings
    3.4. Coming to terms with Death

Module Two
*Relationships and Community*

4. Personal Relationships
    4.1. The Importance of relationships
    4.2. Helping each other
    4.3. Attachment and trust
    4.4. Spiritual companions

5. Community
    5.1 Living in groups
    5.2 Badges of membership
    5.3 Individualism and conformity
    5.4 Telling our story

6. Forgiveness and Reconciliation
    6.1. Guilt
    6.2. Reconciliation
    6.3. How to forgive
    6.4. The challenge of forgiveness

Module Three
*Spirituality and Religion*

7. Sin and Salvation
    7.1. What is 'Sin'?
    7.2. Hard and Soft Sins
    7.3. Christ and Human Liberation
    7.4. How We Benefit?

8. Suffering and Wholeness
    8.1. Suffering
    8.2. Health and Healing
    8.3. Wholeness
    8.4. Wholeness in Society

9. Self and God
    9.1. God and Ourselves
    9.2. Finding God Within
    9.3. God: Words and Reality
    9.4. God and Desire